THE HAPPINESS EFFECT

CREATING HAPPINESS IN AN UNHAPPY WORLD

STEPHEN T. RADENTZ

Copyright © 2021 Stephen T. Radentz

All rights reserved. The use of any part of this publication reproduced, transmitted in any form or by any means, electronic, mechanical, photocopying, recording, or otherwise, or stored in a retrieval system, without the prior written consent of the publisher is an infringement of the copyright law.

Legal Disclaimer

I am not a doctor. I am not giving health advice. I am just giving you some basic facts about natural food and positive mindset. The information contained in this book is for general information and educational purposes only. It does not constitute medical advice. Therefore, any reliance you place on such information is strictly at your own risk. Please check with your medical doctor before starting or changing your medical routine.

Paperback ISBN: 978-1-7365930-7-3
Hardback ISBN: 978-1-7365930-8-0

ACKNOWLEDGEMENTS

I must thank my wife and kids for bringing me more joy than they know, and for giving me a reason to live. Thank you!

Also, my mom and dad who never gave up on me, and taught me the phrase "Whole gob lot." My brother and sister who have always been there when needed. Thank you!

I would also like to thank my co-workers who never seemed to mind my negativity, and taught me so much about diets, cosmetics, and life. Thank you!

To all my friends, you have all helped me become who I am today,

Mary for suggesting I read THE SECRET, and listening to me as I worked out my theories. Gina C, for advising me to write a book, and her husband Jimmy C for allowing us to use the boat that day. The Pleasant Drive crew, you all are the best! And to so many others that have been a part of my life, making me who I am today. Thank you!

Finally, to my editor, and ARCHANGEL INK, my design team, who came through with perfect guidance, and understanding, and a great look. Great job, and thank you!

THANK YOU!

CONTENTS

INTRODUCTION 1

SECTION 1:   THE SETUP 9
1   HAPPINESS HAPPENS   10
2   THE BASICS   14
3   MY STORY   19
4   PLANTING THE SEEDS   24

SECTION 2:   HEALTH ISSUES 33
5   OUR CURRENT HEALTH SYSTEM   34
6   THE AMERICAN HEALTHCARE SCAM   37

SECTION 3:   HEALTH SOLUTIONS 45
7   WHAT ARE PROCESSED FOODS?   46
8   YOUR THREE LIFE CENTERS   51
9   NATURE PROVIDES BALANCE   56
10   FOOD FOR GOOD HEALTH   58

SECTION 4:   NATURAL FOODS 65
11   EATING NATURALLY   66
12   FRUIT   70
13   VEGETABLES   79
14   HERBS   89
15   MISCELLANEOUS NUTRIENT BLASTS   98

SECTION 5:   CANNABIS & HEMP 105
16   THE GREAT CANNABIS CONSPIRACY   106
17   CANNABINOIDS AND YOUR ENDOCANNABINOID SYSTEM   111
18   CBD FACTS   115

SECTION 6:   MOVEMENT OUTDOORS   119
19   YOUR BODY NEEDS MOVEMENT   120
20   NATURE THERAPY   123
21   GARDEN THERAPY   127
22   A QUICK REVIEW   130

SECTION 7:   POSITIVE THOUGHTS   133
23   YOU CONTROL HOW YOU FEEL   134
24   YOU CONTROL YOUR CELLS   140
25   GRATITUDE FEELS GOOD   146
26   COMMUNITIES AND SOCIAL LIFE   149
27   STOP WATCHING THE NEWS!   153
28   REWRITING YOUR STORY   159

SECTION 8:   FINAL THOUGHTS   165
29   FINAL REVIEW   166
30   PUTTING IT ALL TOGETHER   170

INTRODUCTION

Depression kills millions of people worldwide every year. It is consistently listed among the top ten causes of death in America. Nearly 70% of Americans are overweight, yet, at the same time 71% of Americans feel that they are healthy. This contradiction is one reason why this book is needed. Many people simply do not realize how unhealthy and unhappy they are. I certainly was not aware of my destructive lifestyle until I was lying in the hospital unable to keep food down. A lifetime of abusing alcohol and drugs as well as poor diet choices led me down a path to opioid addiction, bleeding ulcers, and depression. My life was filled with negativity.

As I slowly recovered in the hospital, I met a holistic doctor who showed me a different path I could take if I wanted to live a more satisfying life. I had a great family, good friends, and a decent life. I decided that I wanted to give it a try. I didn't simply want to live a decent life anymore; I decided I was going to live my best life.

I was fifty years old, and I knew it wouldn't be easy. However, I decided to set my intention to succeed, and then committed daily to taking whatever actions I needed to correct the mistakes I had made so that I could start living a healthier, happier, and more abundant life. I felt a strong desire to show my family and friends that creating a better life based on natural health, positivity, and gratitude is not only possible but essential to experience abundance and satisfaction.

Over time, I began receiving the rewards of my decision. I became the healthy, happy, and abundant guy that I desired to be. You will hear how everything, including my finances, relationships, and career, improved as I committed to this new lifestyle. You probably won't feel immediate changes in your life simply because you read this book. I know we all want instant gratification; however, I have learned that letting life work at its own pace, without us forcing things along, provides a better outcome for us. Just like it takes time for a seed to sprout and grow into a strong plant, it will take patience and persistence for you to achieve your dream. Having pointed that out, let me assure you that miracles *do* happen, and many of the lifestyle and mindset hacks I share have the potential to improve your life immediately.

According to a study conducted in June 2020, by the National Opinion Research Center of the University of Chicago, only 14% of Americans consider themselves happy. That is some very depressing news. Here we are, one of the wealthiest nations in the world, and only 14% of us are happy. Why is that? I believe it is partly because we tend to allow outside influences to direct our happiness. We also eat excessive amounts of unhealthy processed food, and when your body and mind are unhealthy, your life will also become unsatisfying and *unhealthy*.

During the final editing of this book, the world was seized by a pandemic. Life became extremely scary for many people. Our normal routines were disrupted in a monumental way. One day you have a career, and the next day your job is gone; suddenly, your future is unknown, and you have very little control over your life. At the same time the fears associated with catching (or spreading) a deadly virus created additional worries, which can be devastating to your body and mind. During the lockdowns and the political turmoil surrounding the pandemic response, crime was rising, the number of suicides – as well as domestic violence and drug abuse cases – was increasing, while child welfare was declining. Things were looking gloom. It's no wonder that happiness has become so elusive.

There is a key to activating what I call the happiness effect – your ability to find happiness even in an unhappy environment. The secret is in creating a more holistic lifestyle that embraces nature, positivity, and gratitude. A cool thing about embarking on this path is that you do not have to introduce major disruptions to your life. You simply need to make some minor adjustments to start the ball rolling. Take small steps at first, as every step will build your confidence as you learn that you are in control of your life. Over time, as you consistently reinforce the three life principles – nature, positivity, and gratitude – your best life will begin manifesting itself, and you will be creating the happiness effect. You will also be spreading happiness to others. Soon, you will become the catalyst for everything in your life, and thanks to you, others will be positively affected as well.

I wrote *THE HAPPINESS EFFECT* for you, the 86% who are not happy. As I analyzed my transformation from unhealthy and unhappy into a healthy, happy, and abundant person, I discovered that by embracing nature, positivity, and gratitude, and cementing those three principles into the foundation of my life, I was able to overcome almost anything that life threw at me. Challenges did not disappear; however, I was now in control over how much those challenges affected my life. With a strong foundation built on nature, positivity, and gratitude, you are in control of your body and mind, giving you the ammunition to fight off disease, both in your body and your mind.

Getting my health right was the first critical step I took in my journey toward a better life. You will learn about my health challenges and successes later; however, I will tell you that embracing nature in our food and medicine is instrumental in improving and maintaining good health. But simply eating fruit, vegetables, and herbs is not enough, we must also get outside and embrace our connection to nature. Instilling nature in your life is step one – the missing link to complete homeostasis.

You will hear me say this again and again, "We are a part of nature, we are nature." Creating a strong connection to nature in your food, your medicine, and your environment will have the dramatic impact on your happiness that you are looking for.

The simple equation for a balanced, healthy, and happy life is:

Get your body right.

+

Get your mind right.

=

Get your life right.

I have learned that being healthy isn't enough to ensure our happiness or satisfaction with life. You must also take care of your mind. The great thought mentors throughout history have all stated, "We become what we think." Or put another way, "Where our thoughts flow, our lives will go." I believe that our mindset is responsible for at least fifty percent of our health, and when we are healthy and utilizing positive thinking techniques, we activate the happiness effect, becoming unstoppable. Once activated, your positive attitude will allow you to begin living your best life, with little effort.

The book is divided into eight sections, making it easier to revisit an area of your life that needs more focused attention. As you progress through the book, you will be able to build on what you have learned in the previous chapter(s).

The first half of the book focuses on helping you create a natural environment for your body to thrive in. With personal stories, and scientific studies, I will demonstrate how your current food and medicine may not be improving your health. I will guide you to more natural alternatives which have the potential to heal you and maintain your good health without creating unnatural, unwanted side effects.

I want you to understand the harm that processed food and synthetic medicine may be causing you. The more you know about your diet and how society encourages you to make poor choices, the better you will be at making the best decisions regarding what to eat and how to medicate. Once you have completed reading this book, you may become the community source for natural food alternatives.

The second half of *THE HAPPINESS EFFECT* focuses on getting your mind right. Remember the secret equation?

Get your *body* right,
to get your *mind* right,
to get your *life* right.

Once we have worked on your body, improving your health naturally, it's time for us to study positivity and gratitude. Throughout the book I encourage you to do your own research. Take the facts and theories that I share with you and dive deeper so that you can fully understand the concepts and incorporate them into your life. Educating yourself will also build the confidence you need to overcome the negative influences in your life.

When I discovered the "law of attraction," which simply states that positive thoughts attract positive experiences, and negative thoughts attract negative experiences, I decided I needed to test it for myself in various ways. Being from Missouri, the "Show-Me State," I needed personal verification that it was real. One weekend my family and I were taking a trip to some property we owned in North Florida. Whenever we visited it, it was too hot or too cold, we had lots of miserable cleaning chores, and mostly we didn't have fun. This was our dream property, and all we did was bitch and complain the whole time we were there. Does that sound familiar to you? Have you planned great times only to complain during the entire event? I'm sure many of you can relate.

On our next trip, I set an intention to have a great time. I visualized a casual, stress-free five-hour drive and a weekend full of happy activities. I set my mind to positivity, and the next step was to simply let it happen without worries or fears.

The first thing I observed was that our drive to the property was perfect. Slow cars moved out of my way, the traffic was exceptionally light, and we had some great family conversations. Then, as we got to our destination, everything was working out in harmony. My sons enthusiastically bush hogged the overgrown terrain. My wife and I enjoyed planting garlic and lavender crops and several butterfly attractors. Everyone was having fun. It was certainly hot, being August in Florida, however, it simply was not part of our awareness. At night we sat around a campfire discussing life and laughing at the silly things that families do. We saw several shooting stars and made wishes after each one.

As the weekend came to an end, I sat quietly for a couple of minutes and took time to visualize a stress-free return trip. Once again, all went better than planned. I became convinced that our thoughts dictate how our life goes. The law of attraction works.

From that weekend on, I began paying attention to as many thoughts as I could. We have an estimated sixty thousand thoughts a day, so obviously it's impossible to guide them all. I discovered that the thoughts that truly matter are the ones that we attach emotions to. In general, positive emotions will bring you positive experiences, but the reverse is also true. Your job is to commit to focusing your thoughts on the positive side of life. It's not always easy, however, the better you become at it, the easier your life will become.

The strongest positive emotion you can have is gratitude. Being grateful immediately activates the happiness effect, as even science proves that it is impossible to be grateful and unhappy at the same time. Learning to be grateful for everything will expand your abundance exponentially. Later you will read about the science behind why it is critical to embrace positivity and gratitude if you want the perfect life. For now, take a few seconds and feel grateful for something in your life, allow that thought to bring a feeling of happiness into your body. Cement that happy feeling into your subconscious mind. This little trick will bring you happiness in the darkest of times, because once that feeling is attached to your subconscious mind, you will always be able to bring it back whenever you need it.

As I finish up writing this introduction, I am watching a bright red cardinal, perched on a branch. Its presence takes my mind away from writing as I allow its song to fill me with joy. There is a slight breeze, and on this hot muggy summer day, it is greatly appreciated. Sitting in one of our county's parks is my connection to nature today. I am grateful that our government has provided this place for me to re-connect my body and mind to nature. Nature, positivity, and gratitude are all necessary to live in complete homeostasis, or balance. This is how we can remain consistently satisfied with our life.

I need to thank my friend Gina for suggesting that I write this book. I think she was simply asking me in a polite way to stop sharing natural health and positivity hacks that day while we partied on a sandbar in the intracoastal waterways of South Florida. I tend to get long-winded, and maybe it was time for the conversation to move along. Thank you.

She is not alone in receiving my gratitude. My family has always been there for me, and they may not have believed fully in this project or my ability to pull it off, but they never discouraged me from trying. Thank you. There were countless coworkers, neighbors, and casual acquaintances that have helped me get to where I am today; healthy, happy, and abundant. Thank you.

Finally, I must thank you for purchasing this book. My desire is to assist as many people as possible to achieve more consistent satisfaction with their lives. I believe that if you are confused about your life, and you can't quite grasp the happiness you desire, this book will help you not only get on the path to a better life, but to maintain your best life permanently. My intention is to increase your level of happiness, which will then spread to others as well. When you are healthy and happy, abundance flows more easily and more excessively into your life. I hope this book will bring you closer to your dreams. My wish is for you to learn, continue learning, and then share that knowledge with others. By sharing our knowledge we can make a difference in the world. If we all learn to activate our happiness effect, there will be eight billion people in the world smiling at each other.

Thank you!

SECTION 1

THE SETUP

"No one is in control of your happiness but you; therefore, you have the power to change anything about yourself or your life that you want to change." - Barbara DeAngelis

1
HAPPINESS HAPPENS

When you hit that brick wall, and you can't seem to move due to the despair you are feeling, what do you do? As the bills are mounting and the pressures of life are beating you down, how do you rise above them and succeed?

Many of us look for happiness in shiny, new, expensive things. How long did you own that big screen TV, car, or home before you wanted a new one? The happiness that we feel when acquiring new things is fleeting. When you go through life chasing happiness through the acquisition of things, you will never be completely happy and balanced.

The key to consistent happiness is to create a strong foundation for life by embracing nature, positivity, and gratitude. In this book you will learn how to create your foundation so that when life throws you a curve, you will be able to stand up to the challenge and hit the home run you desire. You will learn how to create your own happiness effect.

Happiness doesn't grow on trees or spring up from the ground, and it is not something that you can buy at the store. Yet, in our constant search for happiness, we spend millions of dollars on books, tapes, and seminars that teach us how to become more satisfied with life. I personally have spent countless hours and dollars on acquiring more and more information on health and happiness, then I tried to put into practice much of what I had learned – unsuccessfully.

I observed incredibly healthy eaters who were frequently sick because they were always focused on negativity. On the other hand, I know people who wake up beaming with positive energy; however, their bodies are always sick due to their poor diet. These observations made me re-evaluate my perception of life. I realized that there is an unequivocal connection between our diets, our thoughts, and the natural world around us.

You may be thinking that this is just another self-help book that won't fix any of your issues. However, this could be the last book on happiness that you need, because it will set your life's foundation, improving your health by embracing nature, while guiding you to find positivity and gratitude for all your life circumstances. You will learn that when you feel healthy and happy, abundance flows easily into your life. It happens every time.

The idea of not having enough money is why most of us are dissatisfied with our lives. We have been brainwashed to believe that money will solve all our problems. You might be saying to yourself, "Everyone they show on television with money appears happy; for example, the Kardashians appear pretty happy as they lounge by their pool." However, money alone does not make you happy or content with life. You can still be miserable even if you are wealthy.

Having lots of money and expensive toys can make it easier to create happiness, and life can be a little more enjoyable. But as you know, having things is not the answer. When your favorite pet or a loved one dies, your health fails, or you don't have any family or friends, you immediately forget how good the material things made you feel. When challenges in life knock on your door, money won't make you smile anymore. You must first find happiness inside of yourself, and then abundance will follow. Guaranteed.

What is it about happiness that is so elusive? Why aren't we all running around with goofy grins on our faces? We all want to be in a state of bliss, so why aren't we? Why do we pay for books, videos, and seminars searching for the source of joy? Why is it so hard to find consistent happiness? What is happiness?

According to Merriam-Webster's dictionary, 'happiness' is "the state of well-being and contentment." Happiness is an emotion, a feeling. And who controls your feelings and emotions? Only you! Your mind controls your emotions, good, bad, frustrated, relieved, tired, alert, joyful, angry. I could stop writing this book right now because the key to happiness is you! There you have it. The secret is out: the only thing stopping you from being happy is you. That fact alone should fill you with joy and positive thoughts.

We are our thoughts. What you think about today, you will become tomorrow. When you learn to control your thoughts, you will become a psychic. You will know exactly how your life is going to turn out. You will know that you are going to be healthy, happy, and abundant, because only you can determine your satisfaction with life.

I was once asked, "How can I make my kids happy?" That is a great question, and the answer is simple. You cannot make someone else be happy. Your children will have to learn how to create happiness for themselves, and they will. However, there is a secret that you can use to help your kids or those around you to become and stay happy. Are you ready to hear it? Here it is: When you decide to be happy with yourself and live your life with a positive and grateful attitude, your kids (and most people around you) will want to be like you.

Many times, when I go to the store, I set an intention to be nice to whoever I run into no matter what. This is going to sound crazy, but when I do this, everyone in the store smiles at me and says hello. If I do run into a negative person, a light-hearted response and a big smile usually creates a positive and friendly exchange.

People will be attracted to your happy mindset. It's an amazing feeling! Suddenly, you will notice that most people around you are in a good mood. Your optimism becomes contagious. Your enjoyment with life becomes a happiness magnet to those around you. Your positivity will bring good things to you and to those you love. This is what I like to call the happiness effect.

The universe is designed to provide you with abundance. My belief is that there are only three life principles that you must embrace to receive the gift of abundance. The first piece of your foundation, or life principle, is to get your body and mind healthy by embracing nature in your food and medicine. If your body does not have the natural nutrients that it needs, it cannot function properly. Every time you put unnatural (processed) food or medicine into your body, you are creating unnatural side effects. This causes your body to work twice as hard to keep you healthy and balanced. Also, your mind will never function at 100% while it is dealing with unwanted chemicals. When your brain has all the natural nutrients that it needs, you will be more positive, and you will be able to see the solutions to your challenges more clearly. More on embracing nature in later chapters.

The second life principle is to embrace positivity in every experience. Throughout this book you will learn simple mindset tricks and life hacks that can turn negativity into a positive experience. Becoming an expert at finding the positive side of everything and then being grateful for the experience will have an enormously positive impact on your life.

The third life principle is that you must be grateful. You must be grateful for everything you already have and everything that you want to receive in the future. As you will learn, our gratitude becomes a magnet for more reasons to feel grateful. As you begin to feel grateful, even for your negative experiences, you will begin seeing abundance flow into your life.

Nature + Positivity + Gratitude = A Healthy, Happy, Abundant Life.

That's all there is to it. It sounds super simple, and it will be with practice. By embracing nature, positivity, and gratitude, you begin to set the foundation for the happiness effect, and not only will you have a happier and more satisfying life, but those around you will also be positively impacted by your example.

"To keep the body in good health is a duty, otherwise we shall not be able to keep our mind strong and clear." - Buddha

2
THE BASICS

There are many age-old tricks that you can implement to create the happiness effect, allowing you to feel happy every day. These hacks have been written about for thousands of years, and many of today's self-improvement gurus continue sharing these techniques. That is what I will provide for you in this book: proven techniques that create happiness. You will learn that getting into nature, even a small city park, or sitting on a balcony with a plant on it will begin to heal you mentally. You will also understand that what you put in your body determines how you think and feel. I will explain how our healthcare system is a great business model that keeps you sick and on drugs, and how our food is connected to the pharmaceutical companies.

You will discover that your body has three areas that need to be balanced so that your life can also be balanced. These are the three Life Centers. Check out Chapter 8 to learn how maintaining these three areas guarantees good health and a balanced, happy life. Chapters 12 through 14 cover valuable health information on a variety of fruit, vegetables, and herbs. This information will assist you in creating a placebo effect of good health.

You will also discover how cannabis and hemp assist our bodies to reach homeostasis and why you need cannabinoids to be balanced. I ask that you keep an open mind while reading these chapters. They are not about getting high; instead, they focus on the history of use and the natural nutrients our bodies receive from the plants. We will also discuss the science behind the fact that all living things are connected and made up of the same stuff. Finally, you will begin to understand that by being thankful – I mean *intentionally* and *emotionally* grateful for everything – you will become happy. It is impossible to be negative and grateful at the same time.

You must understand that the quest for health, happiness, and abundance will take some practice. It will require you to make simple adjustments to your diet and possibly your lifestyle as well. At first, it may seem like hard work, but you must have patience, take daily actions, and soon the shifts will become positive habits that empower you to achieve anything you want out of life.

You will need to focus your thoughts on positivity every day, even when things get challenging. You should know that it will take some time to retrain your brain to see the positive side of things when negativity seems to be everywhere. After deciding to break free of my opioid addiction, it still took a full year and some setbacks before I was able to overcome the addiction and live a drug-free life. Please don't expect things to change magically overnight. Although sometimes, with the right mindset, miracles do happen.

Many of us don't even realize how negative we are. You might be smiling, saying, "I'm the happiest person alive," while at the same time you are screaming and cursing at the car that just cut you off. If you were the happiest person alive, you may try to understand why you were cut off instead of immediately showing anger. Maybe the driver's wife is in the hospital, or their kid needs them right away. These are the types of thoughts that we need to embrace instead of the negative emotions of anger and hate. When the happiness effect is fully in your life, small things like this will have less effect on your attitude, which will make you healthier and happier.

If you're like me, you've spent your entire life being negative and you don't even know it. It will take some time and effort on your part to reverse what you, your family, friends, and the mainstream media have been filling your head with. It may take up to a month or more before your thoughts begin seeing most events in your life with a positive twist. Luckily, science tells us that it only takes thirty days to form a habit, and once you make something a habit, it becomes much easier.

You must practice being positive when failure is staring you in the face. You must learn to recognize the negative feelings that you have, understand why you feel that way, figure out how to learn from your feelings, then decide to see the negative as a positive. If you fall and break your leg, you must be grateful that it was only one leg and not both. Always look for the good in every situation (check out Chapter 23).

Why is it that people find it easier to be negative than positive? Negativity is rampant in the media, so one of the first steps to happiness is… turn off the television (see Chapter 27)! Once you turn off the television, step outside in nature, put healthy natural foods in your body, and start being grateful for everything, the negativity will quickly disappear. Your life will feel enchanted. When you wake up with an attitude of positivity, you'll be looking for the good in everything. This is referred to as an "attitude of gratitude." When something or someone starts to bring you down, you must find a way to turn the experience around. You must try to make it a learning, growing, or simply a positive experience.

When I began my journey to better health, happiness, and abundance, there was a lot of mental work required. I had to change fifty years of negative thoughts. I used to be the guy who woke up saying, "Life sucks and then ya die." But embracing the thought that life sucks only guarantees that your life *will* actually suck.

Once I seriously began focusing on positivity and good health, it took me about thirty days to begin seeing changes in my life. Thirty days to positively change your life is not a long time, and it really wasn't hard to do. However, it did take a firm commitment, and I needed to set an intention every day, even when I didn't feel like it, to be positive and grateful.

I'm not saying that all was perfect after only a month. Like you, I am not perfect, and there are days when negativity is difficult to avoid. I have had many setbacks, and like you, I still face challenges today. However, by changing to a mostly natural-food diet, medicating with nature, and shifting my thoughts to positivity and gratitude, I have become a happy guy, and abundance flows easily into my life. My life has become extremely satisfying! And yours will, too.

Throughout this book I will compare our lives to nature. We are a part of nature, and the similarities between us is rather uncanny. I would like you to think of your journey to happiness as if you were growing a plant. You plant the seed, you water it, you feed it, you talk to it, you nurture it, and eventually you get a beautiful plant. Nature takes its time to create perfection. As you are a part of nature, it will take some time for you to reach your full potential.

You will be forced to overcome obstacles before you can see and feel permanent results in your life. It should be comforting to know that nature also faces challenges that could cause it to fail – for example disease, drought, and humans. Much of our environment is out of our control, so you will need a strong mindset to succeed. Even if you follow every lifestyle shift that I share with you, you will still be tested every day. But if you follow the guidance in this book, you will be able to rise above your challenges and receive the abundance and happiness you deserve, and the life that you desire.

You are taking a giant first step by reading this book. When you start to change your diet to an all-natural one (or mostly natural, as we all need some cheat days), you will begin to be mentally ready for all challenges. When your body and mind are naturally balanced, you will find that life becomes easier, and you simply need to direct it where you want it to go. You must:

Fix your diet,
to fix your mind,
to fix your life.

It is ALL connected, and it is ALL about being balanced. You and all things in nature have been designed to work in a perfectly balanced state. Your body and mind want to reach homeostasis. This book will help you get there. I know you can do it.

Another easy way to bring more happiness into your life is by sharing. As we share with others, we are creating a positive connection to them. This is another example of the happiness effect. As this book begins improving your life, please share this information with others. The more people who hear these thoughts, the happier our planet will be. Think about it. If we all change to a healthy and grateful mindset by activating the happiness effect, there will be eight billion goofily grinning people living life in perfect harmony. That is such a cool thought.

"Every adversity, every failure, every heartache carries with it the seed of an equal or greater benefit." - Napoleon Hill

3
MY STORY

I am not a doctor or a scientist, nor am I a physicist, dietitian, or herbalist. I am not even a college graduate. I have worked as a loss investigator for twenty-five years, where I was paid to observe body language and human nature, then take my observations and determine what someone's intentions were.

I am still an avid observer of people and the world around me. I have researched how nature and our lives work together to support each other. For several years I have studied the health benefits of fruit, vegetables, and herbs, and how their nutrients work naturally to balance our bodies without us doing anything other than consuming them. I have studied with master gardeners, who taught me about the nutrients that plants need to survive and how to successfully combat plant challenges naturally. Through this intensive self-education, I became a master grower and an avid home gardener.

I have studied with some of today's best positive thought mentors – Tony Robbins, Brendon Burchard, Mel Robbins, and many others – as well as studying historical thought mentors – Socrates, Hippocrates, and others – learning the importance of creating and maintaining positive momentum in our lives. We are solely responsible for how our lives play out. This may sound harsh, it might even sting a bit, however, if you're not happy, it's your own fault. I hope to change that for you.

Over the last several years, I discovered the secret to a great, healthy, happy, and abundant life, and I will be sharing my secrets with you soon. I am a born-again nature dude who believes in a universe of possibilities, a greater power, or a creator, a source of all things, and I believe quantum science is beginning to prove that we are all connected at an energy, or vibrational, level. We are all here for a purpose, and I believe that purpose is to grow by learning and experiencing life, while supporting every other living thing.

The information I am sharing has worked for me, but you might need to adjust parts of the plan because even though we are all connected, we are also different. Each one of us needs to follow our own path. My diet won't necessarily work perfectly for you. You need to be in touch with your body and learn what your needs are. When you become familiar with what your body needs for balance, you won't feel like you are making sacrifices in your diet, because when your body gets what it really wants, you will feel balanced and happy. Get to know your body and mind; the answers to a perfect life are already programmed into you.

Let me tell you my biggest health downfalls so you will know that like you, I'm not perfect. I smoked cigarettes for forty years, starting when I was twelve years old because I wanted to be cool like the older kids. But smoking is not a cool thing to do. I spent thirty-plus years as a heavy drinker and partier, having abused most "party" drugs from the seventies and eighties.

However, today I try my best to eat and medicate naturally, while striving to stay positive, grateful, and open-minded. I try to allow the universe to unfold before me, without forcing things to happen. I will drink a bottle of Mt. Dew occasionally, and I also eat a breakfast sandwich from a fast-food restaurant a couple of times a month. But I no longer take synthetic drugs other than an occasional aspirin. I have not taken a pharmaceutical prescription drug since 2016. That's exciting!

I drink an alcoholic beverage about ten times a year. Maybe three times a year, I get sort of "toasted." Otherwise, stopping at two drinks is my routine. You should know that alcohol is extremely hard on your body and mind. Even for you, professional drinkers out there who scoff at hangovers, your body and mind take a big hit when consuming alcohol, and excessive drinking can be a slow and painful death sentence. It is highly recommended that you limit the amount of alcohol you consume.

In 2004 I slightly fractured my spine and broke three ribs falling while cleaning a swimming pool. The pain was intense, and I think my pride was hurt as well. I felt old for the first time in my life. Since I still had to work a physical job, I was given hydrocodone for the pain. I have had a couple of surgeries over the years, and I had taken opioid pain relievers before, but never for longer than three weeks at a time. This time it was different.

One beautiful sunny day, I was working outside, cleaning swimming pools. I had been taking pain medication for about thirty days. I was prescribed hydrocodone, Prozac, and Soma, and I can remember thinking to myself, "I feel so good right now. I want to feel like this every day." From that day forward, I was hooked. I wanted to be a drug addict. I wanted the feeling that I got from taking opium without thinking about the long-term negative effects.

And guess what happened? I became a drug addict. Ask, believe, receive – it works for both good and bad! Although this book is not about recovering from drug or alcohol addiction, it could be used as a starting point. With the information I am sharing with you, everything is possible!

For the next twelve years, my addiction to legal opioids spiraled out of control. All the drugs I was taking were prescribed by my team of doctors. I was a legal drug addict. At one time I was on five different opioids, as well as stomach, nerve, and anti-depression medication. This is what happens when taking prescription pain relievers. You start wanting more, as the pain never goes away, so your doctor prescribes stronger and even more addictive drugs. I was prescribed 1080 pills a month, and I was only forty years old.

During this time, I would over-medicate because I mentally felt that

I was always in pain, and by the end of the month I would run short of pills. I would fight off withdrawal for a couple of days until it was time for a new month of meds. I have smoked cannabis since 1976, and now it was a way to reduce withdrawal symptoms. However, at the time, I didn't make the connection that cannabis is medicine. In Chapter 17 I will teach you why cannabis (marijuana) or hemp should be a part of everyone's diet. Not for a high feeling, but for its health benefits.

For years I was on a roller coaster ride of drug and alcohol-induced highs and lack-of-drug lows. This lifestyle was killing me. After some years, the drugs did not really help any longer, and I never felt good. In the meantime, all this abuse was taking a serious toll on my body and mind, which was only made worse by my diet. Most of my food came from the refrigerator section of the grocery store and fast-food restaurants. If I couldn't microwave it, I didn't eat it. Fruits and vegetables were not part of my diet.

During this time, my doctors never suggested that I should stop taking opium and start eating healthily. Nope, my doctors would consistently want to increase my dosage of opium or prescribe additional pharmaceutical drugs. You will soon learn my beliefs regarding how our healthcare system changes your body. Once you are on synthetic drugs, you will always need more.

After my second week-long stay in the hospital for what turned out to be corrosive, bleeding ulcers, I knew I needed to change something, or I was going to die in a painful way. However, I wasn't mentally ready to stop taking painkillers. Then one night I hit rock bottom. After playing with my prescription dosages and trying unsuccessfully to beat my withdrawal symptoms, I realized that I hadn't planned for my end-of-month drug cutback. With only a couple of pills left, I drove to a pharmacy where I sat in the parking lot, working up the nerve to go in with a gun and rob the place. I planned to steal all the hydrocodone and whatever else they had. I just couldn't face another week of withdrawal.

After about a half hour of sitting in my car, staring at the building, something in my head clicked and I knew I had to change. I was scared that I was seriously thinking about stealing prescription drugs. Thankfully, there was no crime committed that day.

I knew that change would be a challenge, maybe even painful. But it had to happen.

"Plant seeds of happiness, hope, success, and love; it will all come back to you in abundance. This is the law of nature." - Steve Maraboli

4
PLANTING THE SEEDS

My journey to better health began one Christmas day while I was still popping pain relievers. I received a smoothie maker from my family, and I began having a fruit and vegetable smoothie every day. My body went into shock; I hadn't eaten much of anything natural for thirty years.

I also began growing my own herbs, fruit, and vegetables on a 16-by-16-foot townhouse patio. Growing plants has turned into a passion, helping me to learn about natural cures for our body, mind, and life. It has also taught me, as I have said, that we have remarkably similar nutrient needs to plants – shocking, I know. Our cells work similarly to the way plant cells function, always seeking out the best avenue to create a perfect life. Plants keep us safe by preventing illness and disease naturally, providing beneficial nutrients to our bodies. I believe that the reason our bodies work much better when consuming natural ingredients is because we are a part of nature… we *are* nature.

Let me stop for a second and tell you that gardening was, and still is, my therapy. I had to wake up every day to ensure my plants were taken care of. This was especially true with growing cannabis. I needed to be focused every day – even during the withdrawal pains – to ensure a healthy crop was grown. Without having that need to nurture my plants every day, I'm not sure I could have stayed away from the pull of pharmaceutical drugs. Get into growing things! It is extremely therapeutic! (We will touch on the subject of garden therapy later in this book.)

Since 2015, I have been living a more holistic lifestyle, eating more natural foods, drinking herbal tea, and using herbal "health" lotions. I have extensively researched, and I continue learning about how our bodies need a balanced foundation to ensure a more satisfying life. (More on this and the three Life Centers of your body in Chapter 8). When you give your body and mind the natural nutrients they want and need, you will become balanced. When you add positive thoughts and gratitude to the mix, you become unstoppable. Your body and mind can then reach a perfect state of homeostasis, and that, my friends, is where the magic lies. A naturally balanced body and mind will help you to create the happiness effect.

On May 10, 2016, I finally conquered my addiction to opioid pain relievers. I also mostly stopped drinking alcohol. I do have an occasional beer or cocktail socially. If you can control the urge to splurge and limit yourself to just one or two drinks, go for it. I would rather sit around, share some cannabis, and talk big thoughts. But unfortunately, that is not widely accepted in our society.

Today, nearly seventy-five percent of my food is natural and comes from organic sources. I prefer grass-fed, no hormones, no antibiotics, and non-GMO (genetically modified organism) meat. Although it is more expensive, the health benefits are worth the additional cost as we'll discuss later. When eating out, it is difficult to find good meat at medium and low-price range restaurants, so always get some veggies with your chicken, steak, or burger.

I drink around sixty ounces of homemade herbal tea every day. You can find my booklet, *Five Herbal Tea Recipes to Balance your Life*, online for some of my favorite tea blends and their health benefits. Most days my tea contains Tulsi (holy basil, an amazing herb, a favorite of mine), lemon balm, St. John's wort, rose petals, or rose hips as a base. Then I add four or five other herbs to help a specific area of my body: echinacea or elderberry during cold season, bilberry to help my eyesight, or maybe some lavender to keep me calm on a stressful day.

Let me also say that it's not just about what you put *in* your body. It is also what you put *on* your body. I use a homemade anti-aging, moisturizing, rejuvenating lotion made with ten essential oils, including frankincense and myrrh. These two amazing herbs will create synergy when combined, and they have been used for millennia to heal and balance the body. They have the potential to prevent, or reduce, many health issues thanks to their anti-inflammatory and anti-aging properties. My healing lotion also contains oil infused with cannabis. I then blend in shea and mango butter, beeswax, honey, and fresh aloe vera. It is an awesome all-natural healing lotion!

About a year into this more holistic life, my body and mind were returning to what I would call normal. I was feeling better every day. For the previous ten years, I had been depressed and ready to die. This new feeling of health brought with it a refreshing feeling of positivity. I wanted to live again, and I began looking forward to each new day. This will happen for you too as you introduce natural nutrients into your diet.

I craved knowledge of plants as food and medicine, and I dove into the research, learning everything I could. Most of what you want to know can be found online, however, you must filter out the not so accurate sites if you want to get to the truth. You really must read a few articles of opposing views to understand the issue. I suggest that you find at least three articles that are similar, yet not simply copy-pasted. Then, find a couple of opposing views before forming an opinion of how factual the information is.

During this learning phase of mine, a coworker told me that I needed to read *The Secret* by Rhonda Byrne, which is based on the law of attraction. (Thanks, Mary!) Although the law of attraction is only a small piece of the puzzle to a balanced life, *The Secret* is a great book with quotes from many of today's new thought mentors, as well of historical philosophers and religious sources. Maybe my mind was just in the right place at the right time because I began forming a theory about how the universe works. The secrets to a better life began making sense to me.

Shortly after reading the book, I decided to give the law of attraction theory a try. At that time, I was driving a 2006 black Ford Mustang. Driving on the interstate was one of my greatest sources of stress and anger. When a slower car would get in my way or refuse to pull aside, I would fume until I could speed around them. When I could pass, I would stare menacingly, or flip the person off. Yes, you could call it road rage.

One of my first experiments with the law of attraction was that I decided to relax before starting my drive, and to set an intention that my drive would be a stress-free experience. I visualized driving down the highway with clear roads ahead. I even came up with the mantra "Green lights and open roads." Then I took several deep breaths and turned my drive over to the universe. Guess what happened? Today, my drives are always stress free. If a slow car does get in front of me, a safe way around it is usually provided within a couple of seconds. I simply relax and let my intentions happen, relying on the universe, or God, to take care of the rest.

Another super easy beginner trick is to visualize finding the perfect parking spot when going out. Many positive thought books will tell you to try this experiment. The key is to simply set your intention to find the perfect parking spot when you are beginning your trip. Then visualize yourself pulling into that perfect spot. This simple mindset hack seems to work all the time. You will be amazed at how often parking becomes stress free. If the first couple times you are unsuccessful, don't give up, just keep trying. And don't forget to thank the universe, or your God, after your intentions are given to you.

Today, I no longer stop and mentally set my parking spot or stress-free drive intention, because it is now a habit. The universe knows what I want and what I expect. I almost always find great parking spots without having to drive around endlessly.

The reason I am bringing this up is because you can eat the

healthiest food in the universe, but if you don't fill your mind with positivity, your body will still pay the price. The reverse is also true; if you are the most positive person, yet, you eat an unnatural diet, you will never feel balanced. It is all connected! You must have a healthy body, in order to have a healthy mind, in order to have a healthy life. This simple phrase keeps me focused on what truly matters, which is the body-mind-nature connection.

- You must eat healthily.
- You must think positively.
- You must have dreams.
- You must have a happy reason to wake up every morning.
- You must be thankful for everything that you have today and be grateful for everything you are going to receive tomorrow.

Gratitude, as you will learn, is a critical step in creating the happiness effect. Gratitude becomes a magnet for more grateful feelings. I encourage you to even be grateful for that flat tire, because, possibly, it made you late for work, which allowed you to meet the person you end up marrying. The universe always wants you to benefit. Sometimes what looks negative could actually be a good thing for you. To grow and live more fulfilling lives, we must learn something daily. Sometimes the universe will hit us with what looks like a problem at first. But as we learn by working through the challenges and following our gut feelings, the challenges will get solved before you know it, and you will grow more confident. The following story demonstrates how frustrating life can be, and how you can still find a positive in a negative life event.

My life had been about learning lessons the hard way. If you told me I couldn't do something, I would try it anyway. I learned a hard lesson shortly after buying my first piece of property. I'm telling you this only to demonstrate that you need to be able to laugh at adversity. It took me a year to realize it was a useful lesson to learn.

The universe has a way of knocking on your head, hoping you will see the signs, before it punches you in the face. In my past I usually ignored the knocks, gut feelings, instincts, signs, and thus I was regularly punched in the face until I learned to listen.

There was a time when I would ask the universe every day, "When will money not be a constant issue for me?" One day I was feeling particularly frustrated at the universe because not all my bills would get paid that month. While driving home from work, I was practically yelling at the universe for not doing what I wanted. I remember saying, "I am doing everything you said I should do. Why are you not helping?" Almost immediately traffic came to a screeching halt, and for the next thirty minutes, I sat in 90° heat, regretting my attitude. Later that night as I was meditating, it came to me that maybe I was being told to have patience. I decided to let go of the frustration, and within a few months I began paying all my bills every month. Was the traffic jam simply a coincidence? I believe it was more than that; it gave me the answer I needed.

Today I try to realize when the universe is telling me something prior to a full-blown punch in the face. I try to accept that everything will work out for the best. When I simply let go and put my trust in the universe, or God, to create a path toward what I genuinely want, I find that what I want happens – not always the way that I imagined or in the time I expected, but with persistence and patience things generally work out. I simply must continue to take actions to achieve my dreams. The universe needs to know what you really want, and through your emotions and actions, it will know the best way for you to move forward. The journey might not go exactly how you imagine it, but in the end, you will be rewarded for your belief.

The following story is about one of my hardest experiences – I needed to forgive the person who wronged me and find a positive lesson. I also had to come to terms with an $8000 loss because I had ignored the signs that God, or the universe, had been giving me.

My wife and I had saved some money and found ten acres of raw land with a three-acre utility easement on it. Because of the easement, no one wanted the property (maybe they were right?), so the price was a third of what land was selling for. I thought I could plant crops or raise livestock on the easement. I've always wanted to raise goats as they are extremely nutritious and watching them play always brings a smile to my face.

Everything was going great. We had power and water installed. All that was left before moving ahead was to have our fence put up. One weekend while visiting our property we stayed at a horse boarding facility where I was unfortunate enough to meet the caretaker. He was tall and thin like a wrangler, about forty years old, and he talked with that slow country drawl that drives women wild and makes men feel comfortable. He told me about his Christian upbringing and how he never drank alcohol. He also informed me about his fence building ability and how he was an Army veteran trying to make enough money to start his own business and stop caretaking for someone else.

We set up another meeting to finalize details so that he could start building our fence. On the day of the meeting, it was cold and rainy. All we had for protection was a ten-foot canopy, which didn't really help as the rain pounded down on us. The caretaker showed up and was shaking so badly he could hardly talk. He was showing many of the withdrawal symptoms I had become familiar with, but he claimed he was just sick, and again he said he didn't even drink. (Well, maybe he didn't, but he was definitely withdrawing from something.)

I have twenty years' experience as an investigator, I grew up with drug users, and I had been a drug addict. I should have paid attention to the signs. But I was so excited about getting my fence up that all sense of reason left my mind. Instead of listening to the universe, I forged ahead.

That day we handed him a check for $8300. He was so nice and friendly that I never checked references or conducted a background check. As a matter of fact, we only had a "handshake deal." When I read the agreement today, I realize that what he said he was going to do would have cost us twice as much as what he charged us. Too good to be true.

That cold, rainy day was the last time we saw him or my $8300. As my wife and I replayed events months later, she recalled me saying after he left with our check that we would never see him again. However, we laughed it off jokingly, not paying attention to our gut instincts. I was able to catch him on the phone once, and he said he would start working in a week. That was the last time he would answer his phone.

The police as well as the Florida Department of Law Enforcement informed us that because the check was written to a business, not an individual citizen, there was nothing they could do. Apparently, businesses are not treated as harshly as citizens. A citizen would be arrested for theft or fraud. But not a business? The business had filed for bankruptcy, so there was nothing for me to do but to start a civil lawsuit. As the man had zero assets, suing him would accomplish nothing but more stress, anger, and frustration for my family. There was nothing to gain by suing him, which we gratefully understood and finally moved on.

That was an $8300 lesson, which sapped most of our savings at the time. We still don't have our fence, and plans have been put on the back burner for now. We have not given up, just taking a step back to re-evaluate and then move forward. Sometimes it's just the way it is. You must accept your setbacks while planning your comeback. You must keep your dreams alive. Never give up, never surrender.

At the same time, I am grateful to have my property and for learning a lesson without anyone getting hurt. Maybe my pride was smacked, but that has been fixed. I learned to get everything in writing and to always use an escrow account for large transactions. I think you can see that even in a tough situation, there is something good to be found. You simply must look for it. If you learn from setbacks and look for the hidden good, you will not only become a happier person, but you will find that the negative experiences also have less effect on you and your life. Remember this as we begin our journey into natural health.

First, I will try to scare you by sharing my theories on our food and medicine systems. You must first understand the rules of the game. Once you know what you're up against, you will learn how to win.

SECTION 2

HEALTH ISSUES

"Eat your food as medicine, otherwise, you will need to eat your medicine as food." - Steve Jobs

5
OUR CURRENT HEALTH SYSTEM

The first step we'll take toward creating your new life is to get your health under control. To do this, you will need to understand how our health and food systems are currently working against you and how they may be killing you slowly.

Western medicine has a place in our society. Lives are saved every day by modern medicine, but it has become the "quick fix" for Americans. You may have bought into the myth that you need to see a doctor at least once a year even when you are not sick. You do this because your insurance company tells you to just in case you might have a disease and not be aware of it. Well, I can tell you that the insurance company little interest in you being healthy, except that the longer you live, the more money you will make for them. Insurance companies only want to catch cancer early because it will save them money. Our health systems are not necessarily about curing a disease as much as they are about controlling it. They enable you to potentially live longer, however, not necessarily healthier.

You may believe that a single pill will heal you, not realizing that by taking that one pill, you begin creating unnatural changes in your body. I believe that ideal health is possible through nature; however, this takes time and commitment. When you plant a seed (if you have never tried, it's time you did!), it will take a week for your plant to pop up. Then you wait a month, watching it develop. One day you wake up and, BAM! you have beautiful flowers, or fresh fruit and veggies. The point is that for nature to succeed, you need patience. Similarly, when you are healing with nature, it may take a little longer for your body to absorb and respond to the natural nutrients. However, the benefits will last a lifetime.

That one pill you take today will only temporarily make you feel better and is only targeting a small percentage of your body. A nature-based diet will balance your whole body and your immune system naturally, so you won't need a temporary fix. When consuming or medicating with nature, you are creating a healthy, balanced environment for your body. You may even stop going to the doctor because you will not get seriously ill. You may get a cold occasionally; nature gets sick and then bounces back all the time. You are part of nature, so you will bounce back as well.

I have lived a healthcare-free life for many years now. I feel great and I don't feel the need to visit a doctor. We all have our own differing views on this; however, I believe my doctor is there for me when there is a problem, and for now, I don't have a problem. We don't take our cars to the service station unless there is a problem or necessary maintenance, so why do we treat our bodies differently? Frequently, once the shop has your car, they'll let you know of potential future issues, then try to sell you additional services. I feel many doctors treat patients in the same manner. Once you are in front of them, they become salespeople for additional services. Only now you're dealing with your life.

I believe that you can break free from the cycle of doctor, pharmacy, doctor, pharmacy by eating and medicating naturally, maintaining positivity, and being grateful. However, it takes time and dedication. At some point in life, you must choose between dying a slow, painful death by eating industrial foods and taking synthetic drugs, or living a long, healthy, happy, and abundant life by eating naturally grown foods and medicating with nature. The choice is yours.

Your key to good health is not taking a pill for every little ailment. I take about ten aspirins a year for migraine. I take it because my mind believes that it will work faster than drinking a cup of white willow bark tea (aspirin is made from the chemical Salicin, which is found in white willow bark). But in my opinion, aspirin doesn't really work any better. It's primarily a placebo effect.

A recent study from the National Center for Biotechnology Information (NCBI) has shown that a placebo pill works as well as pharmaceutical drugs approximately 45% of the time. It's because many times our minds are just as effective as synthetic drugs. After researching the placebo effect, I realized that for many health issues, you have a better chance of healing yourself using your mind and eating naturally than you do taking pharmaceutical drugs. (Google it. That's a fact!)

If you are eating naturally grown fruit, vegetables, and herbs (FV&H), your mind and body will be able to maintain homeostasis. When your body contracts a disease, you will have the ammunition to fight back. You won't need to take a pill because you have built up a natural defense system in your body.

Having a strong immune system also contributes to you maintaining a positive mindset. You will become fearless in your ability to fight off disease. This confidence will translate into other areas of your life, creating an unstoppable mindset. Your mental attitude, along with a healthy diet will provide you with nutrients to fight off germs, bacteria, and viruses, while keeping your mind sharp and positive. Eating a variety of natural foods will not only keep you away from the doctor, but it will also make you feel happier, creating more positivity in your life, without you having to try very hard. That is the definition of the happiness effect.

"It is very expensive to give bad medical care to poor people in a rich country." - Paul Farmer

6
THE AMERICAN HEALTHCARE SCAM

Next, we are going to delve into my healthcare conspiracy theory. I feel that you need to be aware of how our current food and medicine system works against you. My hope is that once you understand what you are up against, you will be empowered to formulate a plan to improve your health naturally.

Most people predominantly eat commercially processed and packaged foods (CPPF). These, on a good day, only have a high salt and high refined sugar content, very few active nutrients, and some man-made preservatives (from "natural" sources, of course). On a bad day, you may even find dangerous chemicals in them (https://www.hsph.harvard.edu/news/hsph-in-the-news/weed-killer-breakfast-foods/). These high sugar, high salt, chemically synthesized foods push your body into a nosedive toward poor health.

Many dry cereal boxes shout at you from the label, "eight essential vitamins and minerals." However, you're not getting vitamins and minerals from natural sources. Synthetic nutrients are not as complete as the natural nutrients that you can find in an orange, broccoli, or ginger. Since synthetic nutrients also alter your body unnaturally, you need to get some industrial chemicals (also known as pharmaceuticals or prescription drugs) to counteract these effects. This is what I call the cycle of death. Synthetic medicine corrects the unnatural side effects of processed food while creating additional unwanted effects that require more pharmaceutical drugs. It's a never-ending process.

Paying for prescriptions can be very expensive, especially since many drugs need to be taken every day for the rest of your life. But Americans have figured this out. We have health insurance. For approximately twenty percent of your salary, you get one reduced-price doctor's visit a year (even if you are not sick) and you get reduced synthetic drug prices! Yeah… awesome! You get cheap drugs that will eventually create your body's death dance. In my opinion, we only need to carry insurance to cover emergency care and catastrophic issues. Everything else should be treated naturally, and for now, insurance does not cover natural remedies. We should all be asking why.

It is an incredibly sad fact that the unnatural drugs you are prescribed are cheaper than their natural counterparts – the fruit, vegetables, and herbs that will keep you healthy and balanced naturally. How is that possible? Well, many, if not all, prescription drugs are subsidized by the American government, using your tax dollars. While healthy, natural fruit and vegetables get less than fifteen percent of all agricultural subsidies, pharmaceutical companies are collecting billions in government revenue. The other eighty-five percent of government agricultural subsidies (your tax dollars) mostly go to GMO corn, soybeans, cotton, wheat, and sorghum (https://cbey.yale.edu/our-stories/usda-squeezes-the-food-industry-with-outdated-subsidies), which are then converted into processed foods with synthetic ingredients like high fructose corn syrup. Basically, you are paying the companies that are killing you. That is awesome… right?

According to Johns Hopkins University, 250,000 people die from medical errors every year, and according to the *Journal of American Medical Association*, 150,000 people die from adverse effects of prescribed medications each year. That is a minimum of 400,000 people that die every year – 1096 people dying every day! – from mainstream medicine.

I'm sure that you have heard of the opioid epidemic that our government is spending hundreds of millions of dollars on trying to "fix" (your tax dollars hard at work). Opioids kill on average 45,000 people a year in America, and this "epidemic" is in the headlines every day. Yet, no one talks about the 400,000 people – eight times as many as opiate "victims" – who are killed by our healthcare system. Not one single headline swears vengeance on our health system. Nope, no one seems to care. Well, I care, and you should too!

According to the National Center for Disease Control and Prevention (CDC), the leading causes of death in America are as follow. I strongly believe that many of these illnesses can be reduced, or even eliminated, by eating naturally grown foods, medicating with naturally grown plants, and having a positive lifestyle! When you add up the top causes of death in America, potentially three million deaths could be reversed if we all ate and medicated naturally. Check it out:

* Heart disease: 635,260 (may be prevented with a healthy diet)
* Cancer: 598,038 (may be prevented with a healthy body and mind)
** Cigarettes: 440,000 (quit smoking)
** Medical errors: 250,000 (DON'T go to doctors if you're not dying)
* Accidents (unintentional injuries): 161,374 (be careful, pay attention to details)
* Intentional self-harm (suicide): 44,965 (may be prevented with a healthy body and mind)
* Chronic lower respiratory diseases: 154,596 (may be prevented with a healthy body and mind)
** Adverse effects from pharmaceuticals: 150,000 (medicate naturally)
* Stroke (cerebrovascular diseases): 142,142 (may be prevented with a healthy body and mind)
* Alzheimer's disease: 116,103 (may be prevented with a healthy body and mind)
** Alcohol: 88,000 (STOP drinking alcohol)
* Diabetes: 80,058 (may be prevented – or controlled – with a healthy diet)

* Influenza and pneumonia: 51,537 (may be prevented with a healthy lifestyle)
** Cannabis: 0.00 (saves lives)
(* Stats from www.cdc.org; ** Added to list for effect, stats from various government websites, 2017)

As of 2014, it is illegal to not have health insurance in America. This has been stipulated by our government in an attempt to keep us healthy. You get to pay twenty percent of your salary for insurance which covers medical care that may be killing you, and not one single government or medical professional is trying to stop it. No one is telling you these facts. But why would they? It has been a common practice for doctors to get bonuses from the drug companies for prescribing their drugs to you. Your doctor's incentive is not necessarily your health, but to make a higher income. Our doctors have become highly educated and knowledgeable drug dealers. Once you must take a pill for life, there will be more pills to come, and your doctor will continue getting paid, once by you and once by the pharmaceutical company. Great business model.

Let me ask you a question. What happens when you go to your annual doctor's visit? My guess is your doctor finds a slight rise or decrease in blood pressure, or a similar minor issue, maybe a skin spot or two that a specialist will have to look at. After examining you, the doctor shows you some numbers that were found in your blood and urine. These numbers are then used to explain why the doctor needs to prescribe you some man-made synthetic chemicals that you will need to take, possibly forever.

Now, think about this. When you walked into the doctor's office, you were feeling 100% healthy and happy. However, after listening to the diagnosis, you begin to feel that maybe the doctor is right. You start to feel a little less good. You say to yourself, "They are a healthcare professional; they must be right. I must have issues."

The doctor writes a prescription or two that you may not really need, and once you're on the cycle of synthetic foods and drugs, you're stuck. Why do retailers offer you a great sale price on a shirt? To get you in the door to sell you the slacks and belt as well.

The largest chemical companies in the world not only provide chemicals to the pharmaceutical industry, but they are also the largest owners of seeds, fertilizers, herbicides, pesticides, and plant genetics. Based on various online articles, sixty to eighty percent (depending on the source) of the entire agriculture industry is owned by three of the largest chemical companies in the world (Bayer/Monsanto, Chem-China/Syngenta, and DuPont/Dow). The source of the majority of your food is controlled by only three companies, and they also control your medicine. This is a genius business model!

This way, these big chemical, agriculture, and pharmaceutical companies can ensure that you eat what they create. This causes your cells to fail, which then sends you to a doctor, who then prescribes the chemical company's pharmaceutical drugs, which are inexpensive because the government subsidizes them with your tax dollars. It is a win-win for all parties – except for you.

But hold on, there's more to this genius plan. I know you're thinking it couldn't possibly get worse... but it does.

Pharmaceutical /chemical /agricultural companies and the insurance industry giants need a guarantee that their business model will never be heavily regulated. They also need to ensure that the government subsidies keep rolling in to finance their business. But how can these corporations ensure profits and stay unregulated, you ask? By getting their past and current executive directors and other employees elected to high-ranking government positions. Here is the story of Margaret Miller, a Monsanto employee who was hired by the government to review work she did for Monsanto. This is just one example, there are many more found online.

While working as a Monsanto researcher, Margaret Miller contributed to a scientific report for the FDA on Monsanto's genetically engineered bovine growth hormone. Shortly before the report was submitted, Miller left Monsanto to work at the FDA, where her first job was to review the same report! Assisting Miller was another former Monsanto researcher, Susan Sechen. Needless to say, under Miller's guidance, the FDA accepted Monsanto's findings, which became the basis for its approval of Monsanto's genetically engineered bovine growth hormone and its decision not to require labels on milk produced using artificial hormones (https://www.organicconsumers.org/).

I am simply sharing this so that you can decide before agreeing to consume synthetic drugs and processed foods. Hopefully, you can see that you need to become educated about your food and medicine. Then it is up to you to take the actions that benefit you most.

The problem is that synthetic chemicals only make a specific change or target an extremely specific part of the whole body. For example, a drug for your liver may only change one enzyme. This is great for receiving an FDA approval, because the FDA must only look at that particular enzyme in your liver before approving the drug. However, there is little thought to how changing one enzyme can alter the rest of your body. This one little drug might begin a chain reaction in your body, and before you know it, you must take several different pharmaceutical drugs just to stay alive.

Our current healthcare industry treats illness like this: The doctor determines that you have high blood pressure, then prescribes a drug to lower it. However, that drug sends your cholesterol through the roof, so now you need an anti-cholesterol pill, which causes your left foot to swell. Now you need an anti-inflammatory pill, which causes your right eye to twitch, so another drug is needed, and so on. This terrible cycle can only lead to a slow, painful, drug-induced death.

Wouldn't it make more sense to take a more holistic approach and eat a variety of natural foods, thus eliminating the dependency on man-made drugs and chemicals? When you eat an orange or kale, you get a variety of nutrients that work naturally with your entire body. As we are a part of nature, it simply makes sense to let nature help our bodies in a more positive way, without creating unnatural, unwanted side effects.

Commercially packaged and processed foods have the same effect as pharmaceutical drugs. The synthetic chemicals used to create the food products alter your body's natural functions and chemicals. GMO plants are grown using the same company's chemicals (great business model, remember?). These chemicals (e.g., weed killer) have been found in our food. Even though the amounts of these chemicals that have been found in processed food is minute, after years of ingesting them, I believe they are creating negative effects in our bodies. You then need to medicate with synthetic drugs to fight the changes that synthetic foods create. It's a terrible cycle to be on.

I'm not saying that pharmaceutical, agricultural, chemical, and insurance companies are bad because of their business model. All these industries have also saved many lives. GMO crops have made it possible to feed the world (cheaply). Chemicals have made our lives easier, and pharmaceutical companies spend billions of dollars developing drugs that are safe for most people. Insurance helps make basic medical care and catastrophic care more affordable for the average person. These industries also give millions of dollars to social and charitable causes. Thank you! But don't forget that they are in business to make money the best, most efficient way possible, and they are exceptionally good at that!

SECTION 3

HEALTH SOLUTIONS

"Research has shown that even small amounts of processed food alter the chemical balance in our brain." - Marilou Henner

7
WHAT ARE PROCESSED FOODS?

What are processed foods, you ask? Basically, processed foods are any food that is altered in some way. Of course, I also 'process' foods when I make jelly, canned green beans, or even a cannabis tincture. However, I do not use man-made synthetic chemicals or non-organic ingredients in the process. Basically, all processed foods are manufactured products that are designed to have a long shelf life through the addition of preservatives, coloring, and flavorings, and they may contain other unhealthy chemicals.

As GMO seeds ensure a more robust harvest, less loss from pests and disease, GMO corn and soybeans are grown inexpensively compared to other crops. These crops also receive more agricultural subsidies, guaranteeing a profit to the agricultural company for growing them. GMO corn and soybeans can then be turned into any packaged food product cheaply.

The problem, as I see it, is that GMO seeds are grown using these companies' hazardous synthetic chemical fertilizers, herbicides, and pesticides. As recently as February 2019, there were findings of the Bayer/Monsanto Roundup weed killer chemical Glyphosate™, as well as the Dupont/Dow chemical pesticide Chlorpyrifos™, in boxes of crackers and other packaged foods (https://www.theguardian.com/us-news/2018/apr/30/fda-weedkiller-glyphosate-in-food-internal-emails; https://www.ehn.org/when-safe-may-not-really-be-safe-2621578745.html). It should

WHAT ARE PROCESSED FOODS?

also be noted that Monsanto has been successfully sued for covering up knowledge that Glyphosate™ may cause cancer (https://www.nytimes.com/2019/05/13/business/monsanto-roundup-cancer-verdict.html).

Wow, that was a shock, right?

Some processed foods are better than others, but they all contain a lot of refined sugar and a lot of salt. Also, many commercially processed and packaged foods (CPPF) claim to contain "natural" preservatives without mentioning that the nutrient had been synthesized in a laboratory. Which, in my opinion, is not natural at all.

The least nutritious foods seem to be frozen dinners and snacks, chips, cookies, almost anything boxed or canned, sodas, and fruit juice with sugar added. Fast food restaurants, median and low-end chain restaurants have mostly low nutritional value foods as well. However, they are slowly adding more healthy, organic options. I believe this trend will continue as we become more educated about our food.

When I refer to "refined sugar," I am not talking about fructose, glucose, and sucrose naturally found in fruit and vegetables. I am referring to the white sugar extracted from sugar cane, sugar beets, or high fructose corn syrup made from GMO corn. You can find high fructose corn syrup listed in a lot of CPPF, usually as one of the main ingredients.

What is sugar, and do we really need it? Sugar is a carbohydrate that helps create energy in your body – the kind of energy you see when kids are running around screaming and then come to a sudden halt and crash. It gives you quick energy, but that artificial high will also bring you down fast, totally unbalancing your body. Other than creating a short burst of energy, there are no other nutritional benefits to sugar extracted from beets and sugar cane. The only benefit of refined sugar is that it tastes sweet. That's it. Your body doesn't need it at all. All the sugar you need is found in fruit and vegetables. If you need a sugar buzz, eat some berries.

Many people believe that there is a connection between refined sugar and cancer cell growth. I believe from my own research and observations, that there *is* a connection, however, science has currently not proven it. Adding refined sugar to a bad cell is similar to adding nitrous oxide to an engine or fuel to a fire. If they are provided with easily available food like refined sugar, cancer cells have the potential to continue dividing and conquering your good cells at an accelerated rate. Does it make you wonder why cancer rates in America started rising as the popularity of CPPF increased? You should reduce your refined sugar intake today!!

Another downside to CPPF is salt (sodium chloride). The body needs salt as a conductor of energy between cells, and it helps our central nervous system to operate in homeostasis. It also helps in regulating fluids in our bodies, as well as supporting our muscles to work more efficiently.

If we need sodium chloride in our bodies, and salt is a natural substance, then why is it harmful for us? The problem is that consuming excessive amounts of salt increases the chance of getting clogged arteries, which contributes to high blood pressure. High-salt diets have also been related to a higher risk of getting stomach cancer, the fourth most common type of cancer (https://www.ncbi.nlm.nih.gov/pmc/articles/PMC2682234/). Traditional table salt has also been refined, thus removing many of the natural nutrients that could assist your body. Therefore, kosher, and other specialty salts are a better choice.

We only need about one quarter teaspoon of salt daily (575 mg). There is a group of indigenous people in the Amazon rainforest, the Yanomami, that eat as little as 200 mg of salt daily, and they live long happy lives with low blood pressure and almost no cardiovascular health issues. We should all take a page from their playbook and reduce our salt intake.

Americans consume over 2500 mg of salt a day on average. One can of vegetable soup, which is marketed as a "healthy" food, could be killing you – it usually contains around 1000 mg of salt! If you have high blood pressure and poor circulation, limiting salt intake will aid in cleaning and strengthening your arteries, as well as improving your entire cardiovascular system. Reducing your salt intake will give you a healthier life while assisting in maintaining homeostasis.

Fruit and vegetables generally have low amounts of sodium in them naturally. If you feel the need to flavor your meal, you can sprinkle salt lightly (the keyword, folks, is *lightly*) on your natural food. However, if you do not add any to your diet, you should have more than enough to sustain your body just from eating natural foods. There is research being done confirming the health benefits of Himalayan salt, which is reported to contain up to eighty-four nutrients. The most noticeable differences to table salt are that it has not been refined, and it is pink. When using Himalayan salt, you are getting all the nutrients that nature provides.

I have started drinking eight ounces of distilled water with a pinch of Himalayan salt first thing every morning. Many people will add a slice of lemon as well. This daily ritual seems to refresh my body and help wake up my mind. Our bodies are made up of sixty percent water and integrating water into our bodies after sleeping assists our cells in staying active. I feel it gives my cells a natural boost first thing in the morning. It's my way of saying thank you to my cells for keeping me alive overnight. This way my body wakes up in a happy, natural way.

Health hack: Using garlic, celery, or onion salt instead of iodized salt gives your body the awesome health benefits of onions, celery, and garlic too.

Briefly, we need to talk about lotions, sunscreens, and most cosmetics. These products are also commercially processed with synthesized chemicals. These gooey, fragrant concoctions are contributing to your skin cell death. By applying that thick goo to your skin, you are causing skin cell suicide. (Good thing skin cells regenerate in about twenty-seven days. You still have time to save your skin!) If you believe blocking the sun's beneficial rays from entering your body by adding a thick layer of petroleum and alcohol to your skin is good for you, I disagree.

Yes, some UV rays can be harmful during long-term exposure. However, getting outside is one of the most therapeutic activities there is. Most of us are not getting enough sun. Your skin knows what it needs, and it will adapt to your environment. If you get outside regularly, your skin will be prepared for the sun's rays. If you apply aloe vera before and after being in the sun, your skin will thank you for the moisturizing and other healing benefits. Also, aloe vera will not clog your pores, unlike many commercial sunscreens which have some nasty chemicals in them. Let your skin shine! (Of course, within reason! Anything in excess is harmful.... Duh! :)

If you have ever read the ingredients on the box your cosmetics come in, you will understand what I'm referring to. Many of the ingredients are words we can't pronounce, let alone know what they are. I suggest you research some of the words and learn what exactly you are applying to your skin. In many instances you are using a blend of petroleum oil. Yes, that black gooey stuff they pull out of the ground. You know, the stuff that runs your car. Yes, they "refine" it, but still, I just can't stop seeing your body covered in black tar. Yuck! You are filling your pores with crude oil, alcohol, and synthesized plant material. I don't know about you, but it sounds creepy to me!

I hope I haven't scared you too much as that is not my intent. My hope is that you will start educating yourself on how your current way of eating and medicating is affecting you. Your awareness of how processed food, in combination with synthetic medicine, may be killing you will assist you in building confidence when making your future diet and medicine decisions.

"Health is a state of complete harmony of the body, mind and spirit." - B.K.S. Iyengar

8
YOUR THREE LIFE CENTERS

Now I will describe three critical areas of your body that you must take care of. This information is based on observations of myself and others who I believe are living balanced lives, as well as those living in chaos. If you follow my advice and do everything you can to ensure these three areas of your body are cared for, you will automatically trigger the happiness effect. I call these areas the Three Life Centers.

Our bodies are made up of vibrating energy. Most, if not all, religions talk about the *life source* or the *life energy* within us. You may have heard of the seven chakras. These are the energy centers of your body according to the Hindu religion. The chakras are centered on you vertically, and they function as "healing centers" for your mind and body. Many people believe that by altering the chakras, they can improve their health and their life.

For you to be in perfect, balanced harmony, your entire body must be in sync. That sounds like a daunting task. You have a lot of organs and other critical areas in you that will need your attention. Even breaking down your body into seven chakra energy centers is a lot to focus on. To make your journey to health and happiness as simple and easy as possible, I have broken our body down to only three critical areas of focus. The cool thing is that most fruit, vegetables, and herbs affect these three areas naturally by design. The universe always has our backs!

THE THREE LIFE CENTERS

1. The gut (stomach, kidneys, liver)
2. The chest (heart, lungs, blood circulation)
3. The head (brain, thoughts, central nervous system)

As you can see, the three Life Centers encompass all your major organs that make life possible. Without any one of these three areas, you would most certainly die. Let's take a closer look at each. Remember that I am not a doctor, so my explanation of how these areas work is in general terms. Nevertheless, the information is fully accurate, even if it is explained in an unscientific way. I just want to ensure that anyone can understand the points I'm making.

Life Center # 1: The GUT – Stomach, Kidneys, Liver, Immune system

The gut is critical for digesting food and sending fresh, healthy nutrients out to the rest of your body. Your stomach processes all the good and bad stuff that you eat and drink. It sends the processed nutrients to your other important organs (liver and kidneys), where the nutrients are cleaned up and sent to support your blood and other cells.

This Life Center is where your nutrients' journey begins. When you are feeding your gut healthy, all-natural foods, you are creating a natural environment for the rest of your body. In my opinion, it is easier for your stomach to digest natural foods than synthetically processed foods. Your body will have less toxins to remove, which makes the digestion process run more smoothly. Naturally grown foods are designed to work with our bodies without creating unnatural, unwanted side effects, whereas artificially processed foods will alter your body in an unnatural way.

When your gut takes in unhealthy, unnatural foods, the rest of your body may not get the nutrients that it needs. Your body must first remove the man-made toxins before it sends out the nutrients. Many times, the toxins avoid detection and will begin creating cancers. If you overload your gut with junk, the kidneys and the liver get overworked, and they begin to fail. This will then affect the second Life Center, the chest, which also affects the third Life Center, your head. This then affects your ability to think rationally; you get depressed, and life goes downhill rapidly. Luckily, our bodies are extremely resilient, and once we begin receiving our nutrients from natural sources, our bodies can begin the healing it needs.

Life Center # 2: The CHEST – Lungs, Heart, Circulation

This is just as important as the other two Life Centers. This is where your life is maintained. Your heart pumps freshly cleaned blood to every area of your body. Your lungs pump fresh oxygen into your blood. Your body needs fresh oxygen and clean blood all day, every day. Your heart and lungs never stop working for you, but they cannot do their job without proper nutrition. When you have the nutrients you need from Life Center # 1, you will ensure optimal functions of Life Centers # 2 and 3.

Your solar plexus is also in this area: just below your rib cage and above your belly. It is an area of spiritual energy in many religions and meditation practices. This is where your "gut feelings" come from. If you haven't already realized this, all three Life Centers react to this "gut feeling." Your stomach tightens up, your heart beats a little faster, your mind is racing, and maybe you even feel a little dizzy. Trust your gut feelings, they are a complete body-mind message that you need to listen to.

When your first two Life Centers are depleted due to a poor diet, you get less nutrients to your brain. If your brain doesn't have the nutrients it needs, it begins to fail. All three Life Centers must be balanced for you to reach homeostasis.

Life Center # 3: The HEAD – Brain, Thoughts, Central Nervous System

Your brain controls all life functions. This is the master control center of your body; this is your computer. The crazy thing is that your brain controls your Life Centers subconsciously. You don't need to continually think about taking a breath, it just happens naturally. In Chapter 24 you will learn how your mind controls your cells, giving you the ability to heal without using synthetic drugs. However, if your brain doesn't have the right amount and variety of nutrients it needs, it will stop functioning. And if your mind is unhealthy, your body will not function properly either.

Have you ever noticed that when you are tired, hungry, or sick, you have trouble thinking? Being tired and malnourished makes it much harder to stay positive. The Navy SEALs learn this during their initial training: after a week of diminished nutrition and sleep, they have extremely reduced cognitive abilities. The only way to keep your mind healthy is by keeping your body healthy. It's all about balance.

Your thoughts form in the brain. As many historical philosophers have said, "You are what you think you are." You control your life through your thoughts. Your thoughts can, and do, make you sad, happy, sick, frustrated, joyful, etc. You – and only you! – can control your thoughts. You – and only you! – control how you feel. We will talk more about this in later chapters.

All three Life Centers work together to keep you perfectly balanced. You are a part of nature, and just like a plant, if just one nutrient is absent, it affects all other life functions. If a plant's roots are depleted, it affects the rest of the plant. Without enough water, light or nutrients, the plant begins to die. When one of your Life Centers is missing what it needs, it will begin to drain the other two. As it becomes harder to find the nutrients you need, all three Life Centers will begin failing. To avoid a total breakdown, our bodies need to become and stay balanced.

By embracing the body-mind connection, you are creating homeostasis in your body, your mind, and your life.

But how do you maintain the perfect balance between the three Life Centers? By the things you put in your body and mind! Put your seat belts on because you're going to learn the secrets of a happy, healthy, and abundant life, starting with improving your natural health.

"Look deep into nature, and then you will understand everything better." - Albert Einstein

9
NATURE PROVIDES BALANCE

Before we jump into what you should be eating, let me explain how I see nature providing everything that every living thing needs. A tree in the forest has every nutrient that it needs and will survive without our help and without moving for hundreds of years. You are a part of nature. The universe provides everything you need, every day.

Think about each individual continent on planet Earth. Now visualize how nature provides every nutrient that every living thing needs on that continent. Yes, there are areas around the world that have limited supplies. However, I feel that if our natural resources were better managed, you could find the plants and animals on each continent that contain all the nutrients that a human being needs to live in perfect homeostasis. Yup, if all people had to survive on their continent alone, with no interaction with other countries, they could. Nature, or God has placed everything we need within our grasp, and when used responsibly, our needs will be met for years to come.

Another great example of how nature, or the universe, provides for us is the story of rain. As a master grower, I love a good rain shower. Every time a plant receives water from the sky, they will grow greener, fuller, and taller. Would you like to know a secret? Rainwater is basically H2O. Yes, it can accumulate chemicals in the air as it falls, however, it is just plain ole water from the sky. From my observations, this water from the universe benefits plants better than any man-made fertilizer.

Nature provides everything you need for health and happiness in abundance. We simply must educate ourselves on how nature works with us. Then use this knowledge to maintain our health and happiness.

One of the best ways to learn about nutrition for your body is to start gardening. Plant nutrient needs are remarkably similar to human nutritional needs. Plants need nitrogen, oxygen, potassium, phosphorus, and other minerals, a multitude of micronutrients, water, light etc. When a plant has all that it needs from its environment, it will grow big and strong. Just like us, silly humans.

However, when a plant is deficient in just one nutrient, things start to go wrong. For example, a plant without potassium will not develop fruit or flowers, leaves droop, and the plant eventually dies. The human body is the same. If you stop receiving potassium in your diet, your muscles will no longer contract, and your heart will begin beating erratically, which reduces circulation. You will become sleepy, and you will eventually die.

What happens if you add too much potassium to a plant? That's a great question as well. An excess of potassium will begin to block nitrogen absorption, which stops the plant from growing. This then creates other issues that must be treated with additional nutrients. With an overdose of potassium, your body will shut down your kidneys, which will eventually lead to your unnatural death. What I'm getting at is that you need balance in your diet and in your life. Too much or too little of anything creates a domino effect of bad health. The great thing is that nature provides everything that you need to be balanced.

"Let food be thy medicine and medicine be thy food." - Hippocrates, 300 BC

10
FOOD FOR GOOD HEALTH

Fruit, vegetables, and herbs. That's it, the secret is out. The key you have been looking for is that simple. Every day you need to consume naturally grown fruit, vegetables, and herbs (FV&H). Those three little things will allow you to reach homeostasis, the perfect balance in your life. FV&H are instrumental in creating a happy, healthy life because…

If you keep your body happy,
your mind will be happy,
which will allow your life to be happy.

The *big three* – fruit, vegetables, and herbs – will provide almost everything you need to live life in perfectly healthy balance. Each nutrient source provides different, yet similar nutrient benefits. When you combine fruit, vegetables, and herbs by eating a variety of each (variety is the key!), your body will become balanced.

Let me take a second and talk about meat. As you noticed, I didn't include it in the *big three*. Why? The vegan diet is powerful, and vegans have proven that you can survive on a plant-based diet. The key word is *survive*. You are not looking to just survive. You are reading this book because you desire a perfectly balanced life with great health, happiness, and abundance. We will discuss the vegan diet shortly.

The truth is that I am a meat eater, although I fill up on vegetables.

I really love ground beef; I think I could eat a hamburger every day. I would, however, substitute beef with goat meat if the price were reasonable. Goat meat is extremely beneficial for you with its high nutrient and high protein content, without the potentially bad fats from beef. Goats are also mostly organically raised, and the meat generally tastes like beef, in my opinion. Goats take up less space to raise and release less methane into the atmosphere than cows do, which could potentially benefit our environment. Americans consume more beef than any other country, and Americans are near the bottom of the good health list when it comes to wealthy countries. I wonder if there could be a connection...

Have you ever seen the episode of the TV show *Friends* where Joey had "meat sweats"? To this day when I eat low quality meat, I tend to sweat profusely, but when I eat meat without chemicals, I have no reaction. I put the blame on the antibiotics and hormones in low quality meats. This is why I try to only eat naturally fed (grass, free range, or pasture raised) meat without any chemicals, hormones, or antibiotics added.

I prefer non-GMO meat. I'm sure you have heard stories of GMO crops altering your DNA and other horrors. I cannot verify that this is true, however, science is always evolving, and someday we may prove the destructive effects of altering nature. However, my reasoning for limiting these foods is based on the fact that the GMO crops that are fed to livestock have all been chemically treated, so the animal's body is absorbing those unnatural chemicals as well. This tells us that when we eat meat, our bodies could potentially inherit traces of chemicals from fertilizers, herbicides, and pesticides. Also, GMO corn and soybean fed cattle have less nutrient value than pasture-raised livestock. According to Healthline.com: "Conventional grain-fed beef is highly nutritious, but grass-fed beef contains more carotenoids, vitamin E, and other antioxidants." I feel that paying a little more money for chemical-free meat is worth the cost. Better quality meat makes a huge difference in how your body can digest it, which benefits your other Life Centers as well.

I made my decision to continue eating meat because vegans do not consume vitamin B12 and some other minor nutrients in great enough quantities to allow their bodies to reach a perfect balance. If you only eat plants, you will need to take B12 supplements to find balance in your body, which means you will have to take a synthesized, or man-made substance. This one little fact tells me our bodies are designed, or have evolved, to require the nutrients that can only be obtained through consuming animal protein. However, I also feel that we do not need meat in our diet every day. Two to four times a week is probably sufficient.

We, as a society need to figure out how to produce enough meat in a humane way, without using chemicals. Maybe we could try going back to smaller local farms growing crops and raising livestock for their immediate county's use. We don't need to feed the whole world. We do need to feed each other. Just a thought.

Diets and "superfood" fads come and go. When one of these new discoveries is publicized in the media, everyone thinks this will be *the one*. This new super diet or superfood will fix everything – it will create a perfect life. People then jump on the bandwagon and spend a fortune on one superfood or super diet, expecting their life to not only change for the better, but to stay that way without any additional work.

Sure, there are many fruits and vegetables that have more of one nutrient or another. Some plant-based foods really are super, and they can be used to heal a specific area of your body or assist in preventing specific illnesses. For example, a serving of kale has 200% of the recommended daily allowance (RDA) of vitamin C, 300% of the RDA of vitamin A, and 1000% of the RDA of vitamin K, which is great for our blood and helps prevent heart disease and osteoporosis. It is truly a super plant. But it won't bring complete balance to your life.

It is the variety of natural nutrients that we put in or bodies that matters. It is the balance of nutrients that we consume, along with our mental attitude that will bring us to homeostasis. Changing from one super diet to the next only confuses your body, so it will never be balanced. This means your mind will never be balanced either. I can't stress this enough; variety in nature equals balance, which will bring your life to complete homeostasis.

Acai berries, coconut oil, hemp seeds, flax seed, kale, chia seeds, goji berries, tiger nuts – they have all been called superfoods, and at one time they cured everything from hangnails and toothache to cancer and the black plague. Today the super craze is CBD, which is said to be able to cure anything. Well, I'm here to tell you that it cannot. Maybe your mind can heal all things, but CBD alone will not cure all health issues. More on this in Chapter 18.

Along with superfood fads, let me touch on the issue of super supplements. Supplements are basically synthetically made nutrients, combined to give you a power punch of health in a pill. Many supplements that claim to be all natural are simply pieces of plants combined in an unnatural way. When you eat an orange, you get vitamin C, as well as vitamin A, calcium, magnesium, and other nutrients that will work with your body naturally, without creating unnatural side effects. This is because an orange is created in nature, just like you. The whole plant is what keeps you healthy, not pieces of it. Extracting one nutrient from a plant will not create a perfectly balanced body, and putting synthesized supplements in your body won't create a natural feeling of homeostasis. Your body works best when it receives a variety of natural nutrients from a variety of natural sources.

Here's some news that will make you smile: it is okay to cheat occasionally. Life is about balance. If you always eat naturally, then it's okay to grab a frozen food once or twice a week when you don't have enough time to cook. Don't beat yourself up. Remember: Your mental attitude is half your health. Getting upset over going off an all-natural diet is silly. Enjoy your cheat days, enjoy every day!

Your diet doesn't have to be perfect; life is about staying balanced. My diet is more balanced than most people's, however, I have not removed processed food from my life completely. I know that I am consuming a wide variety of natural nutrients every day, thus offsetting the occasional unhealthy food. I know that my body and mind are working in a homeostasis state. I can feel it, and you will too. I also know that I could do so much more, and I strive to do better on most days.

When I feel out of balance, I figure out why, and then I adjust either my diet or my mindset. That's why this lifestyle is so cool. You are in total control. You are the boss of your life, and by embracing nature, positivity, and gratitude, you can have the perfect life.

I seldom eat dessert; however, I do like ice cream and a few times a month I will eat some. I also find myself craving Mt. Dew soda some days, and this is one of my favorite cheats. Did I mention that my soda of choice has one of the highest amounts of high fructose corn syrup out of all sodas? As of this writing, it has about 200 mg of sugar. Yup, and it's also loaded with 60 mg of sodium. When I break the rules, I really break the rules! I am such a rebel.

I seldom snack during the day; I accomplish this by focusing on tasks that keep my mind occupied. After years of observing people, it seems to me that snacking, and the lack of movement are two of the major contributing factors to obesity. I believe that science backs this up as well. If you must snack, fruit and vegetables are your best friends. Yummy, I know. Who doesn't love a plain ole celery stick? Bet you didn't know that an eight-ounce serving of celery has 30 mg of salt, as well as vitamin C, beta-carotene, and twelve different antioxidants (see www.healthline.com).

My favorite snack is fruit. It is sweet, and it provides you with natural sugars and carbohydrate energy. Eating fruit throughout the day, especially if you mix up the colors, will provide you with healthy fuel for your cells. (The color of fruit and vegetables can provide clues to their health benefits. More on this in Chapter 12). Fruit will give you more sustained energy than soda, coffee, or a candy bar. Do you often get tired in the afternoon? Add more fruit to your diet.

Nuts are also a great choice for an energy-boosting snack. Nuts contain an assortment of nutrients including vitamins, minerals, and micronutrients, and they are loaded with antioxidants that can benefit your body. One study found that eating half an ounce of mixed nuts every day can reduce your risk of stroke by half (https://nutritionfacts.org/topics/nuts/).

Life is about balance, that's why you need variety in your diet and your life. There is always a healthier alternative to processed foods. But the super cool thing is that you don't always have to choose it. I have my cheat days, which I offset by drinking sixty ounces of herbal tea daily to help cleanse the adverse chemicals from the processed foods. I balance the good with the better.

Positivity Hack: Notice I did not say I balance the "bad" with the "good"? You should never label something as a "bad" choice. It is simply a choice. Remember that your positive mental state makes up fifty percent of your health. You are always making "good" or "better" choices.

SECTION 4

NATURAL FOODS

"A healthy diet is a solution to many of our health-care problems. It's the most important solution." - John Mackey

11
EATING NATURALLY

How do you ensure that you are getting the nutrients you need? That's the million-dollar question, and the answer is: you need to do some research! This will not only make you feel smarter, but you will also feel great that you have accomplished something for yourself!

I will, however, just for you, share some of my favorite Life Center foods. I'm sure you have heard that the food you eat will determine how well you perform. It's true! What you put in your body determines how well your body works, which then helps your mind work, which determines your quality of life.

First, let's go over a few basics that I feel you should know. The body needs a variety of nutrients every single day. I am not getting into exact daily requirements because, to tell you the truth, we are all different and we all have different nutritional needs on different days. Do I even have to mention that women need higher iron, especially during their menstruation period? You cannot treat everyone the same.

So how do we ensure that when we need more iron, we have it? Or what if you feel a scratchy throat? Do you keep eating the same things or do you change your diet to adapt to how your body feels? If your answer is "If I have a sore throat, I take a pill," STOP IT! Sorry for yelling, but taking a pill is usually not the best thing to do.

If you are already eating a variety of fruit, vegetables, and herbs, your body has what it needs to fight off any disease. There is no need for a pill! When you get sick, your body goes into attack mode, and your cells begin to fight off the germs. Whether you take medicine or increase natural nutrient intake, it will take a few days for your preferred medication to work. The time it takes to get well is about the same with natural and synthetic medicine, so you might as well go all natural and live healthier.

Let's say you have a sinus infection. If you're a mainstream pill gobbler, you'll run to the doctor, pay a hundred dollars, then go to the pharmacy and spend more money on drugs that will change your body unnaturally. The sinus meds, cough syrup, aspirin, and antibiotics take about three days to begin working. If you're lucky, in about a week's time, those pills will help you feel better.

Meanwhile, those same synthetic drugs are altering your body unnaturally. Your kidneys are put under additional stress to remove the synthetic toxins, while your immune system tries to fight off the sinus infection. As stated earlier, pharmaceutical drugs often force your body to work harder. Continually using chemicals to fix health issues will eventually lead you to needing more prescription pills to restore the balance in your body.

Still, you take the pharmaceutical drugs, assuming you'll get well faster. In the example above, it takes a week to feel real relief. But you can also choose to heal naturally in... get this... about three to five days. Yep, about the same amount of time. The best part is that you are working *with* your body, not *against* it. You are creating zero unwanted side effects while you are fighting off your cold using natural ingredients. You are restoring and maintaining homeostasis naturally.

Here's how a sinus infection might be dealt with naturally: You will increase your diet to include anti-sinus, anti-viral, anti-congestion herbs, like echinacea, elderberry, red clover, pau d' arco bark, and pine needles. Black tea and yerba mate tea will give you increased energy. I would also increase vitamin C from citrus fruits, kiwi, goji berry, and don't forget the purple fruits loaded with antioxidants. I would add tomatoes and some green veggies including spinach and kale, and purple veggies like carrots, cabbage, eggplant, and onions. Getting all these items and their nutrients into your body can simply be accomplished by blending them in a smoothie.

As I started to eat a more natural diet, having a daily smoothie allowed me to receive all the nutrients without having to taste the individual ingredients. As I changed my diet, I found that my taste buds were accustomed to sugar, salt, and unnatural chemicals. Natural foods simply didn't taste good to me. This may happen for you as well. It took persistence and a daily intention to improve my health and to become accustomed to food without sugar and chemicals, but it can be done.

I would not eat starchy foods with high gluten content, even though I believe we as a nation have overreacted with our fear of gluten. The body needs gluten in small amounts to maintain balance. Yet, I have learned that it may have negative effects on your sinuses. I would limit the amount you consume. No high fructose corn syrup, no refined sugar either. Why no sugar, you ask? Well, as I said earlier, cancer cells could potentially be attracted to refined sugar. A cancer cell is, for lack of a better word, *disfigured,* and it doesn't perform like your good cells do. The same thing happens when you're sick: you're fighting disfigured cells that got into your body. So, just to be safe, no refined sugars.

In the next couple of chapters, I will go over a few of my favorite FV&H. I'll share their benefits and how they affect your Life Centers. Science is beginning to prove that knowing how a nutrient is supposed to work with your body increases the healing benefits. This is another example of the placebo effect. Your brain has the power to heal. Research has shown that on average, thirty to forty-five percent of all healing can be attributed to the placebo effect. When you combine knowledge with natural food and medicine, you are unstoppable.

When I feel a cold coming on, I immediately begin taking elderberry syrup. I know that the ingredients are scientifically proven to reduce cold and flu symptoms, so I expect to be healed by this natural formula. It works most of the time, and I am confident that my belief in how it should work increases my recovery speed.

My hope is that you will use this information as a starting point for your own research. We all have different needs and likes. What works best for me may not work as well for you. Take this basic information and go learn as much as you can. You'll be an expert on natural health in no time.

"Every time you eat or drink, you are either feeding disease or fighting it." - Heather Morgan, MS, NLC

12
FRUIT

Fruit is my favorite go-to food for snacks and for the health benefits. Even though I love my veggies and herbs because of their balancing effects, fruit is my favorite. Fruit is high in fiber and natural sugar, thus, they are my sugary snack substitute. Fruit also has some heavy antioxidants as well as high vitamin and mineral content per serving, which assists us in fighting off colds, the flu, and cancers.

Purple-colored fruit overflows with antioxidant properties, making them an excellent choice for their anti-cancer benefits. Science is proving that purple fruit and vegetables are amazing at controlling free radicals, giving your body a complete package for cancer prevention.

What is an antioxidant, you ask? Great question. The simple answer is: "Antioxidants are molecules that attack free radicals." A free radical is a molecule that is unstable or deformed. This deformed molecule can attack good cells, and they can also transform good cells into free radicals, causing a chain reaction that leads to cancer. When you think of free radicals, visualize a zombie: A zombie can attack and kill you, or they can transform you into another zombie. Free radicals do the same thing. Attack and kill, or attack and conquer. Either way, you and your cells lose.

If you don't want to become a zombie and die of cancer, you might want to start eating some fruit, especially the purple and red varieties, which also contain phytonutrients called anthocyanins, which are responsible for the purple and red coloring of fruit and vegetables. They also have anti-inflammatory, anti-cancer, and antiviral properties. These little fellows really attack free radicals. I'm sure you've heard the saying: "A purple fruit a day keeps cancer away." Or was it about apples? Never mind. I think you get the idea.

Let us begin with one of my favorite fruits that some people say is a vegetable, and it is actually both. Do you know what it is? Yep, a tomato. The confusion comes from the description of fruit. According to the *Encyclopedia Britannica*, "Tomatoes are fruits that are considered vegetables by nutritionists. Botanically, a fruit is a ripened flower ovary and contains seeds." Thus, tomatoes – just like plums, zucchinis, and melons – are technically edible fruits. As I mix tomatoes into my fruit smoothie, to me, they are definitely a fruit. You may call them whatever you like, just include them in your diet. They have amazing health benefits!

1. TOMATOES *(Solanum lycopersicon)*:

Tomatoes have been around for thousands of years. It seems that the Aztec nation was the first to cultivate them around AD 500. From Central America they were brought to Spain and Italy and eventually became a staple food in many cultures.

Lycopene, a strong antioxidant is one of the standout nutrients found in tomatoes. I've even heard an Italian celebrity chef state that the combination of tomatoes and olive oil eaten weekly has the potential to prevent many forms of cancer. Beside lycopene, there is also a good amount of vitamin A, B6, C, K, as well as beta-carotene, magnesium, potassium, iron, and calcium in it. Tomatoes only contain 10 mg of sodium and 2.7 mg of sugar per a four-ounce serving. I eat the equivalent of five cherry tomatoes most days. Let's see how they help our three Life Centers:

GUT:
- Improves digestion.

- Has probiotic properties to help regulate bacteria in your stomach.
- Improves liver and kidney functions.

CHEST:
- Aids respiratory system.
- Improves blood circulation.
- Regulates blood sugar (anti-diabetes).
- Strengthens your heart muscles.

HEAD:
- Reduces cognitive impairments.
- Improves memory.
- May prevent Alzheimer's disease and dementia.
- Improves eyesight.

Garden Hack: Tomatoes are one of my favorite plants to grow. There is nothing better than going outside to your own garden and grabbing some fresh, ripened tomatoes that you grew. Interestingly, there is a noticeable difference in the flavor of a fruit harvested in the morning versus afternoon or evening harvested fruit. The morning harvested tomatoes will have a sweeter flavor. Try it and see for yourself.

2. BLACKBERRY (*Rubus*):

Here is a fruit that will jump-start your body. It's just another treat that nature has provided us with since the beginning of time. The Greeks and Romans used the plant both as medicine and a food source. The well-preserved body of a woman who had blackberries in her stomach was found dating from over 2,500 years ago.

On my property I have blackberries growing wild. When they are in season, I love finding their hiding spots and grabbing as many as I can. It's so cool to just pop them in your mouth out in nature.

Blackberries make an excellent sweet snack. Not only are they one of the best tasting berries (in my opinion), but they are also one of the most beneficial for your health. They are high in vitamin C (one cup has about 35% of your RDA), they also have high amounts of vitamin A and K, as well as 14% of the RDA of fiber. Blackberries may prevent tumors, as they have anti-cancer properties due to their high antioxidant values. They are efficient zombie cell killers and pack a powerhouse of beneficial nutrients.

GUT:
- Reduces cholesterol.
- Lowers stomach acid.
- Improves digestion.
- Increases beneficial bacteria.

CHEST:
- Improves blood circulation and insulin response.
- Reduces inflammation in arteries.
- Improves lung functions.

HEAD:
- Boosts brain function.
- Improves memory.
- May improve symptoms of Alzheimer's disease and dementia.
- Mood enhancer.
- Anti-depressant.

I love taking blue and blackberries, covering them with warm honey sauce, then pouring them over some vanilla ice-cream. So yummy. Killing cancer cells while eating ice cream. Too cool to be true!

3. BLUEBERRY *(Cyanococcus)*:

Here is another mega-antioxidant! Blueberries are one of only a handful of fruits native to North America. Their use can be traced back to the beginning of Native American history. A fun fact about blueberries is that they were not commercially cultivated until the early 1900s. For centuries, blueberries were simply gathered in the wild.

Today, you can find blueberries at reasonable prices at most grocery stores all year long in America.

They have hefty amounts of vitamin C (24% of RDA), vitamin K at 36% of RDA, and manganese at 25% of RDA. Blueberries also have vitamin A (good for eyesight), iron, magnesium, and potassium. Blueberries pack a punch of nutrients that you need into a small blue ball. Eating blueberries every day has the potential to reduce your cancer risk. These little blue nutrient blasts also contain anthocyanins, which attack your unwanted free radicals. As stated earlier, purple foods are a great source for anthocyanins.

Fruit Hack: Freeze your blueberries at least 24 hours before eating. The frozen berries become super sweet. I've looked everywhere for the reason but found nothing. Some sort of chemical reaction? I don't know the science behind it, but frozen blueberries are sweeter than fresh.

GUT:
- Supports liver functions to improve the removal of toxins.
- Improves kidney functions.
- Boosts immune system.
- Supports digestion.

CHEST:
- Improves circulation.
- Improves lung functions.
- Reduces the risk of cardiovascular disease.
- Protects the lining of arteries to ensure proper blood flow throughout your body.

HEAD:
- Improves memory and cognitive response.
- Has anti-aging properties.
- May improve symptoms of Alzheimer's disease and dementia.
- Improves learning capabilities.

I am incredibly grateful that these little nutrient bombs are now a commercial crop. I love my blueberries and I try to eat them every day, because I know that the knockout nutrients are healing my body, and they taste great.

4. KIWI *(Actinidia deliciosa)*:

This fruit from New Zealand by way of China is also known as the "Chinese gooseberry." Its name comes from the fruit's similarities to New Zealand's national bird, the kiwi, which is also small, brown, and fuzzy.

Kiwi was not available commercially until the 1970s. Look at it now; it's a superfruit. Kiwis contain some major nutrients, such as vitamins A, B6, C, E, and K as well as calcium, magnesium, iron, phosphorus, potassium, and only 3 mg of sodium. The kiwi hits all three Life Centers with a powerful punch of nutrition. This is another fruit I can usually find all year long, and I do eat it on many days.

GUT:
- Aids digestion by increasing the processing of proteins.
- Balances alkalinity in your stomach.
- Reduces heartburn and indigestion.
- Removes toxins and reduces the risk of kidney stones.
- Improves immune system.

CHEST:
- Helps regulate blood pressure and blood sugar (reduces diabetes risk).
- Reduces triglycerides (fat in blood cells).
- Reduces risk of heart disease.

HEAD:
- Repairs damaged DNA.
- Improves cognitive development.
- Improves memory.

- Reduces stress by releasing serotonin (the "happy drug").
- Helps prevent brain defects in babies.

Kiwi has more potassium than a banana, and it tastes a little like strawberry to me. Kiwi makes an awesome addition to any salad, and it is also good with fish. Three kiwis a day may keep the doctor away!

5. APPLE *(Malus domestica)*:

An apple a day keeps the doctor away. That's it! That's the proverb I've been looking for! There is a lot of truth to this, but don't just eat apples. Variety is the key. Apples contain 14% of your RDA of vitamin C, 5% of vitamin K, one to four percent of vitamins A, E, B1, B2, B6, and 6% of RDA of potassium. You also get a healthy dose of fiber.

Apples have been a documented food source for nearly ten thousand years. They are believed to have come from Asia, although they have been found in every ancient culture. It is even said that Eve, the first woman, ate the forbidden fruit that resembled an apple. And how do apples affect your Life Centers?

GUT:
- Improves digestion.
- Improves liver functions by removing toxins from the digestive tract.
- They are also great for weight loss. They fill you up with only about 90 calories per medium-sized apple.

CHEST:
- Improves cardiovascular health.
- Helps in regulating blood sugar.
- Reduces risk of heart disease and clogged arteries.
- Improves circulation.

HEAD:
- Aids in the prevention of Alzheimer's disease and dementia.

- May reduce effects of Parkinson's disease.
- Helps prevent memory loss.
- Reduces the risk of having a stroke.

Apples are a great nutrient-packed fruit that is good just picked off the tree, juiced, cooked with pork, or baked in a pie. Americans grow over 45,000 tons of apples every year. Now, that's a whole gob lot of apples!

5. GRAPES *(Vitis)*:

Grapes have also been around since the beginning of time, and they can be found on almost every continent. The first mention of grapes in the Bible is in the Book of Genesis, the beginning of life. Throughout the Bible wine is mentioned an additional two hundred times. Egyptian hieroglyphics show that grapes were cultivated over 8,000 years ago. The oldest known winery, which was found in Armenia, was built over four thousand years ago. Apparently, grapes and the wine made from them have been very popular for a long time.

Grapes are another great nutrient bomb for your body. I could just copy and paste everything I said about blue and black berries. Purple and red grapes are loaded with antioxidants, which makes them a great anti-cancer food. Green grapes are also full of nutrients.

Grapes make great wine, and some folks have claimed a glass of wine every day is good for your heart. However, a group of Spanish scientists found that the benefits came from the grapes, not from the wine. You no longer have an excuse to drink. Sorry.

Here is how grapes balance your Life Centers:

GUT:
- Contains fiber, which aids regular bowel functions.
- Its antibacterial effects may improve digestion by promoting healthy bacteria growth in the stomach.
- May reduce kidney disease.
- Improves kidney and liver functions.

CHEST:
- Lowers blood pressure.
- Aids in the prevention of heart disease.
- Improves lining of arteries, which reduces blood clots.
- Improves lung function.

HEAD:
- Improves memory.
- Aids in Alzheimer's prevention.
- Increases oxygen to your brain.
- Relieves stress.
- Improves focus.

Grape juice, or should I say, ice cold grape juice (no sugar added) is one of my favorite drinks. The health benefits are off the charts, and so is the sweetness. However, you must be careful because of its high natural sugar content – it's around 40 grams per 8-ounce serving. Just like the other fruit mentioned, grapes have anti-cancer properties and should be included in your diet several times a month when they are available.

I hope you are starting to get a better idea of what your diet should look like. Fruit contains some of the most antioxidant and antibacterial benefits out of all our food. You absolutely must have fruit included in your diet. Now let's move on to vegetables.

"Nothing will benefit human health and increase the chances for survival of life on Earth as much as the evolution to a vegetarian diet." - Albert Einstein

13
VEGETABLES

You may not want to eat your veggies like Momma said, however, you'll be missing out on some amazing easy-to-get health benefits. First, vegetables have very little, if any, cholesterol. As a matter of fact, they generally improve the cholesterol levels in your body as studies have demonstrated (https://pubmed.ncbi.nlm.nih.gov/9160820/ and https://www.pcrm.org/good-nutrition/nutrition-information/lowering-cholesterol-with-a-plant-based-diet).

There are some vegetables that have an incredible amount of one nutrient or another. As mentioned previously, one serving (1 cup) of kale has 1000% of the RDA of vitamin K, and carrots have over 200% of the RDA of vitamin A. This means you can really boost a specific area of your body just by increasing your consumption of a certain vegetable (same with fruit and herbs).

As of 2021 the Center for Disease Control (CDC) recommends three cups of vegetables and two cups of fruit a day. The Harvard School of Public Health recommends nine servings of fruits and vegetables, and the Food and Drug Administration (FDA) recommends four servings of fruit and five servings of vegetables. As you can see, the experts all agree that we need to be eating fruit and vegetables, however, there is no consensus on the exact amounts that we need. To keep it simple, you should eat as many fruits, vegetables, and herbs as you can every day. But please don't go overboard and gorge out just because they taste so good. Moderation and variation are the key to bringing balance to your body.

I recommend that you eat some veggies throughout the day to replenish nutrients as you go. Mix up the colors because each color represents different benefits. Experts say that when it comes to produce, you should eat the rainbow. Next you are provided with a brief history and the health uses of some of my favorite vegetables. Use this information as a starting point for your journey to natural health.

1. KALE *(Brassica oleracea)*:

Kale has been cultivated for more than six thousand years in Asia. Now, it is found on every habitable continent. An interesting fact about kale in America is that up until the 1990s, it was mostly used as a decorative ingredient. Then the nutrient benefits were let out of the bag and, BAM! just like that, kale became a superfood. Kale can now be found year-round in America.

Kale is one of the most nutrient-rich foods on our planet. I was not a fan of the taste the first several times I ate it. However, I have learned that I can blend it with other foods to hide the taste. I can feel a definite difference on mornings when I put kale in my smoothie: I tend to be more alert, focused, and energetic.

Kale contains 1000% of your RDA of vitamin K and over 130% of the RDA of vitamins A and C. It also has 10% of your calcium, potassium, and vitamin B6 needs, one to seven percent of magnesium and iron, as well as micro- and phytonutrients. Kale has a powerhouse of nutrient benefits that will give energy, focus, and balance to your Life Centers.

GUT:
- Builds healthy bacteria in your stomach.
- Aids digestion.
- Strengthens immune system.

- Helps detoxify your liver.
- Improves kidney functions.

CHEST:
- Anti-inflammatory, which helps reduce heart disease.
- Improves circulation.
- Removes plaque buildup in arteries.
- Reduces risk of lung cancer.
- Aids in proper respiratory system functions.

HEAD:
- Improves memory.
- Reduces risk of Alzheimer's and Parkinson's disease.
- Reduces stress.
- Helps maintain homeostasis/balance

Kale has been blamed for causing kidney stones, however, more recent studies have shown this is not true. Don't believe everything you hear or read. Research everything until you know all the facts. (See https://news.medill.northwestern.edu/chicago/kale-sheds-bum-rap-on-kidney-stones.)

Kale provides a plethora of nutrients that we need to survive, and if you only eat one green food, it should be kale! But remember, one plant will not keep you balanced and healthy. Variation and moderation will bring you to a balanced life.

2. POTATOES *(Solanum tuberosum)*:

I am including all varieties of potatoes – sweet potatoes, Idaho, russet, purple, white, yellow, or red. They are all good for you. Earlier we talked about antioxidants and anthocyanin and how those chemicals fight off free radicals, or "zombie cells." Well, here we go again: just as red and purple fruits have more antioxidants, so do red and purple vegetables, including potatoes.

The Inca civilization in Peru were the first to cultivate potatoes around 8000 BC. Potatoes are believed to have been the Incas' primary protein, or energy source. From Peru, the conquistadors took the potato back to Europe. The introduction of potatoes to Europe is credited with a quarter of the population growth between 1700 and 1900, as potatoes provided the extra nutrients to feed the masses for extraordinarily little cost. Today potatoes can be found around the globe in every culture.

Potatoes get a bad rap for causing weight gain. Potatoes have around 163 calories per tater. That's less than the 170 calories my Mt. Dew has in it! Which one is making me fat? Well, I'm here to tell you that it is not necessarily the potatoes that makes you fat! Nope, it may be the way you prepare them, or – this may sound harsh – it could be the amount you eat. I understand how easy it is to overeat potatoes, as I love them too. I also enjoy that they can be prepared in a variety of ways.

First off, many experts recommend that you do not fry them (although I love French fries). Also, you should limit those yummy, high-fat toppings that make them taste so good. Sour cream, cheese, and margarine are great toppings, but they also have unhealthy fats, as well as a lot of salt. You can add toppings like broccoli or peas, or even a little olive oil to your baked potatoes without feeling guilty. However, keep your toppings to a minimum, and let the potato be the centerpiece of the dish. When potatoes are baked, there is only 8 mg of sodium so you may add a little salt (garlic or celery salt would be a better choice), even a little bacon may be okay. Potatoes sautéed in a healthy oil (olive, grapeseed, hemp) is also a great idea. Don't fear potatoes; nations have lived on them and flourished throughout history. Now let's see how they heal your Life Centers.

GUT:
- Contains high fiber to improve digestion and gut health.
- Promotes weight loss by filling you up and providing a punch of nutrients without a lot of calories.
- Promotes good bacteria to aid kidney functions.

CHEST:
- Reduces cholesterol, allowing your heart to operate at a higher level.
- Improves circulation.
- Beneficial for your lung health.
- Strengthens the cardiovascular system.

HEAD:
- Improves memory.
- Improves central nervous system functions.
- Reduces stress and depression.
- Releases serotonin and dopamine.

Potatoes are what I like to call a "happy food," as they release serotonin in your brain, which contributes to your happiness. Potatoes are probably my favorite vegetable and one of my top five foods. I would eat them every day if I could. Don't fear potato calories. When eating them in moderation, you will be better than good.

3. CARROTS *(Daucus carota)*:

WOW! Carrots contain nearly 300% of the RDA of vitamin A: 200% of the actual vitamin and another 100% is converted from the beta-carotene content. Vitamin A is great for the eyes, so carrots will work with your body to help maintain excellent vision. Most people do not realize that carrots are also an amazing anti-cancer food. Several studies have shown that the phytonutrients in carrots reduce the risk of a variety of cancers.

Historical records date the use of carrots to over 5,000 years ago. However, they have only been commercially cultivated since around AD 900 – archeological digs have found evidence of farming in areas near Afghanistan and Iran. Prior to the 1500s, carrots were mostly white, purple or red. Using selective cultivation methods to bring out more sweetness and less core, farmers created the carrot of today, thus orange became the color of choice for consumers. Or was it Bugs

Bunny and his orange carrot that changed public opinion? We may never know.

GUT:
- Aids in detoxing kidneys and the liver.
- Improves digestion.
- Helps control weight gain.
- Promotes good bacteria in the stomach.

CHEST:
- Improves circulation.
- Reduces the risk of heart attack and heart disease.
- Lowers blood pressure.
- Assists in regulating blood sugar (good food for diabetics).
- Regulates cholesterol.

HEAD:
- Has anti-aging properties.
- Improves your memory and cognitive abilities.
- Slows macular degeneration.
- Improves eyesight.

Another great thing about carrot colors, just like with many other fruits and vegetables, is that they show you what health benefits your body will receive from them. For example, orange is full of beta-carotene (eyesight), purple is high in anthocyanins (zombie cell killers), red is high in lycopene (anti-cancer), yellow has lutein (eyesight and anti-cancer), and the dominating benefit of white carrots is that they are high in fiber (weight loss). It is cool how nature identifies plant benefits for us.

Sweet hack: Carrots add a lot of sweetness to a smoothie or a salad, even though they have less than 3 grams of sugar. How cool is that?

4. BEANS *(Phaseolus vulgaris)*:

Beans are one of the earliest known cultivated crops. Early cultures depended on the protein value as well as the ease of growing and preserving them. Beans have been found in the pyramids of Egypt, and it is believed that they were placed there so that pharaohs would have food in the afterlife. Native Americans planted beans with squash and corn – a planting method known as "the three sisters." It is a system that uses the natural growing pattern of the three vegetables (corn, squash, and beans) to assist each other to achieve optimal growth. (You should research this awesome method and then come back here!) If plants can work together to create a perfect growing environment, shouldn't people do the same? After all, we are all part of nature.

Beans and legumes are part of the *Fabaceae* family. Many people substitute beans for meat protein as they have 41 grams of protein per cup, which is the highest amount of protein available in the plant family.

Beans contain high amounts of B vitamins, calcium, iron, magnesium, and vitamin C. They are great for increasing fiber intake, and they are an excellent source of energy. Beans are also incredibly versatile. Soybean is transformed into everything from imitation crab meat, steak, and fried chicken to hamburgers and hot dogs. Soybeans are an excellent source of nutrients for your body. However, around 93% of all soybeans in America are GMO grown, meaning that they could potentially contain synthetic herbicide, pesticide, and fertilizer chemicals. So, you might as well drink Mt. Dew and eat fast food. (Just kidding.)

GUT:
- Improves digestion by promoting beneficial bacteria.
- Provides fiber and protein.
- Improves liver health.
- Strengthens stomach lining.

CHEST:
- Improves lung functions.
- Improves cardiovascular health.
- Improves circulation.
- May prevent heart disease.
- May reduce risk of lung cancer.

HEAD:
- Has anti-aging properties.
- Improves memory.
- Benefits central nervous system.
- Improves cognitive functions.
- May improve symptoms of depression.

Beans are one of my favorite vegetables, and just like potatoes, I could eat them every day. But as I have been saying, it's all about variation and moderation!

5. ONION (*Allium cepa*)

Onions have been used for over 5,000 years. Sometimes they get a bad rap because they may give you bad breath, but onions are amazing, and a mint leaf or two helps with bad breath.

They are considered medicinal in most cultures. I don't know of a single culture that doesn't cook with onions. As a matter of fact, each American eats around twenty pounds of onions every year.

The list of benefits is long, so I will just touch on a couple of big hits. ANTI-CANCER. Did I say that loud enough? Yep, onions have chemicals that fight off those pesky free radicals. As purple onion contains the most antioxidants, if you have cancer concerns, start eating more of them. I love them in my salads!

GUT:
- Anti-ulcer properties.
- Promotes healthy bacteria in the gut.

- Improves digestion.
- Improves immune system.

CHEST:
- Improves cardiovascular system.
- Lowers blood pressure.
- May reduce asthma symptoms.
- Thins blood while regulating blood fat and cholesterol.

HEAD:
- Improves memory.
- May reduce the risk of getting Alzheimer's disease.
- Aids in stroke prevention.
- May prevent Parkinson's disease.

As you can see, onions provide a positive blast for all three Life Centers. The good news is that there are so many ways to consume them. A simple Google search brings up over a million search results. Here is another secret: only peel the dried outer layer of the onion, as the most nutrients can be found in the first skins around the outside of the bulb.

Onions release a chemical that interacts with your tear glands. It is called 'lachrymatory factor,' or propanethial-S-oxide (sometimes called thiopropanal-S-oxide). It is an airborne sulfur-containing organic chemical that is like tear gas (www.chemistryworld.com). The simple solution is… don't hold your head directly above the onion while cutting it. Also, when chopping onions, don't breathe through your mouth, as nose breathing reduces much of the crying effects. You should try cutting the onion away from your body, while you have a fan blowing the fumes away. That should reduce your tears to a small sniffle.

By now you can see the importance of eating vegetables every day. They provide a lot of nutrients for your body, and they don't add many calories. When you are getting your nutrients from vegetables, your body benefits because they work better with your body than synthesized and processed foods. It is recommended that you eat a variety of vegetables throughout the day, replenishing your body as it uses the nutrients.

Now let's jump to herbs. Herbs are some of the most beneficial plants that you can put in your body. I call them "balancing plants" because they really help balance your body, positively interacting with your three Life Centers.

"Ounce for ounce, herbs and spices have more antioxidants than any other food group." - Michael Greger

14
HERBS

According to Merriam-Webster's dictionary, "any plant with leaves, seeds, or flowers used for flavoring, food, medicine, or perfume" is an herb. Also, any seed-bearing plant which does not have a woody stem and dies down to the ground after flowering is an herb too. And which herbs are good for you? All of them! Every herb seems to have a specialty use, like elderberry, echinacea, and red clover for colds, or yerba mate and ashwagandha for energy. But after extensive research I started to realize that most herbs have the necessary nutrients to affect all parts of your body – therefore I like to call them "balancing plants." They are beneficial whether you are using them as flavoring, added fresh to salads and prepared foods, or extracted in tea, tinctures, or oils.

I have already mentioned that I drink about sixty ounces of herbal tea every day. I do this because the herbal nutrients create a positive, balanced environment in my body. They remove toxins and add life-giving nutrients to all three Life Centers. By drinking herbal tea, I am creating good health throughout my day without trying. This also keeps my mind focused because my body is in prime condition and in a state of homeostasis. Thus, herbs help to create the happiness effect.

When adjusting your diet to herbs, always start with a small amount and see how it affects you. We can all be allergic to different plants, so always test first! Remember, you should research everything you eat – don't simply accept what your friends or the media tells you.

When making herbal tea, I recommend changing only one ingredient at a time, then wait and *feel* how it affects you. If all is good, keep on experimenting. The larger the variety of herbs you put in your body, the more balanced your body will become. By ensuring variety, you will have – and will be replacing – the nutrients that you need throughout the day just by having a drink. That is an extremely easy way to maintain good health.

The following group of herbs are what I use as a base for most of my herbal teas. Every herb listed can be used daily with no complications or side effects, except for St. John's wort, which has been documented as potentially creating side effects when taking some prescription antidepressants. However, if you are a mainstream go-to-the-doctor kind of person, always check with your medical professional before taking herbs, especially if you are taking synthetic drugs. Sometimes man-made synthetic drugs don't play well with nature, or nature doesn't play well with altered nature.

Here are a few of my favorite herbs and their main benefits for our health. Remember that mixing up the herbs daily will give you the variety of nutrients that is required for optimum health. In case you haven't heard, variety is the spice of life.

1. ST. JOHN'S WORT *(Hypericum perforatum)*:

Wow! What can I say? This is one extreme balancing herb – it helps to keep your body working in homeostasis. Most herbs have this effect, but St. John's wort (SJW) is a real body-balancing bomb. This mega herb is well known for fighting depression and anxiety. It has been said to be potentially just as effective as the synthetic drug Prozac (fluoxetine), yet, my doctors never prescribed it to me. Why is that?

St. John's wort has been used medicinally for over two thousand years. The Greeks were one of the first nations to document using it in the 1st century. As the Greeks took many ideas from Egypt and other ancient cultures, my guess is that SJW's use as medicine is much older.

The plant has antibacterial, antiviral, anti-inflammatory,

antioxidant, anti-tumor, and anti-cancer properties. It has the potential to reduce menopause symptoms and can be used as a sleep aid. As you can see, St. John's wort is a heavy hitter in the healthy herb category. It hits all major Life Centers with a plethora of nutrition.

GUT:
- Improves appetite.
- Improves liver and kidney functions.
- Stimulates gastric juices and enzymes to improve digestion
- Boosts immune system

CHEST:
- Improves circulation.
- Regulates heartbeat.
- Improves lung functions.

HEAD:
- Reduces depression.
- Reduces anxiety.
- Helps alleviate OCD and stress.
- Enhances your mood.
- Can calm ADHD symptoms.

If you are taking prescription drugs, check with your doctor prior to using St. John's wort, as it may influence your medication. St. John's wort has been documented to improve our liver functions, and sometimes this might negatively react with synthetic medicine.

Also, St. John's wort has loosely been connected to other side effects, like vomiting and diarrhea, however, this is rare. I do not know anyone personally who has had any such issues. It's best to start with a small amount and see how it affects you before jumping in with both feet. I put a teaspoon of SJW every day in my tea for about two weeks, then I take a few days off to ensure my body uses up the nutrients and to help clean out any built-up toxins. I have been using it for several years, and I have never had any negative side effects.

2. LEMON BALM *(Melissa officinalis)*:

Did you know that lemon balm is a member of the mint family? Looking at the leaves, you can see the similarity. Unsurprisingly, it can also be used to freshen your breath. Lemon balm has an amazing smell, and it is also great for maintaining homeostasis.

Lemon balm's prime nutrients are vitamins A, C, iron, calcium, potassium, magnesium, and zinc. Lemon balm has antiviral, antibacterial, antioxidant, antimicrobial, and anti-cancer properties, and it is super beneficial for your central nervous system too. It can be used daily with no known negative side effects; it can make a great stand-alone hot or iced herbal tea. You can cook with it to add color and a soft lemony flavor to any dish. It is easily extracted in olive and coconut oil: soak it for thirty days, and you will have lemon balm-infused oil.

How does it affect our three Life Centers? Let's find out.

GUT:
- Reduces nausea.
- Improves digestion.
- Improves liver and kidney functions.
- Can stimulate your appetite.

CHEST:
- Balances blood sugar.
- Improves circulation.
- Improves lung functions.

HEAD:
- Reduces anxiety.
- Enhances your mood.
- Reduces stress.
- Improves memory and brain functions.
- Improves the functions of your central nervous system.

Lemon balm has been used for over 3,000 years. The Greeks and Romans used it primarily as a medicine and as a spice. The Holy Roman emperor Charlemagne was so grateful for lemon balm's calming effect that he stated that every healing garden should include this amazing herb.

I use lemon balm almost daily for its calming and balancing effect. It relaxes me without making me sleepy. I love the taste of freshly picked lemon balm; it tastes kind of like lemon candy, and it has a sweet lemony scent.

3. HOLY BASIL *(Ocimum sanctum L.)*:

Holy basil, or Tulsi, is part of the mint family (*Lamiaceae*) and is native to India and southeast Asia, where it is used in Ayurvedic medicine. It is an extremely important herb in the Hindu religion. Its origins can be traced back to the very beginning of Hinduism and is directly associated with their gods. Tulsi can be found growing throughout India, both in personal gardens and in temples for its spiritual and health benefits. It is considered the most medicinal variety of basil, and it has been used since the beginning of recorded history.

It is packed with vitamin A and K; two tablespoons of fresh Tulsi contain six percent of your recommended daily allowance of these vitamins. However, when the plant is dried, the vitamin K content jumps to a whopping 43%, giving you incredible benefits for your blood. Holy basil also has good amounts of calcium, magnesium, iron, potassium, and of course, micronutrients and phytonutrients. Tulsi assists in maintaining balanced blood sugar and stress hormone levels. It positively affects the central nervous system and blood circulation. Holy basil also calms your stomach acid, which aids digestion. It will also assist in keeping the respiratory system functioning at a high level.

GUT:
- Calms gastric juices.
- Improves urinary tract.

- Improves immune system.
- Can reduce heartburn and gas.
- Improves liver and kidney functions.
- Aids in the removal of toxins from the body.

CHEST:
- Improves respiratory system.
- Improves blood flow.
- Improves lung functions.
- Improves cardiovascular health.

HEAD:
- Reduces stress and calms tension.
- Improves central nervous system functions.
- Improves memory.
- Improves eye health.

I add this "superherb" to my tea almost every day. I also grow a lot of it because it is easy to grow in warm climates above growing zone 9. It can easily be grown indoors in cooler climates too. It is an excellent balancing herb that affects your whole body in a positive way. This variety of basil has more nutrients than all other basil varieties. This herb is a power punch for your three Life Centers. It is probably the one herb I recommend for daily use. It is so good for you!

4. SAGE (*Salvia officinalis*):

I am sure you have heard of sage, which is primarily used for flavoring meat, most notably our Thanksgiving turkey. But did you know it is also great for your blood, immune system, and bones? It even fights lung cancer! High in vitamin K (great for blood), it also has B6, calcium, iron, manganese and more. Sage is mostly an herb for your chest Life Center, but like all herbs, it hits your entire body with good stuff.

Sage has also been used for thousands of years. Its use dates to ancient Egypt, where it was used primarily for the treatment of infertility. This is another herb that the Holy Roman emperor Charlemagne required farmers to grow due to its medicinal benefits, as well as its use as a cash crop.

GUT:
- Improves digestion.
- Increases your appetite.
- Reduces the acid in your stomach.
- Increases beneficial bacteria.
- Reduces heartburn and indigestion.

CHEST:
- Improves lung functions.
- Reduces risk of lung cancer.
- Improves blood flow by strengthening the heart and cleansing your blood.
- Regulates your blood sugar.

HEAD:
- Improves memory and brain function.
- Reduces effects of Alzheimer's disease and dementia.
- Helps the central nervous system perform at an optimum level.

Sage can also be used as an antiseptic, or antibacterial cleanser. I use it in an herbal bug spray, as well as an ingredient in my rejuvenating lotion. White sage is used in spiritual ceremonies and rituals to cleanse an area. This practice is known as "smudging" and has been performed for centuries. There is more to sage than just seasoning your turkey and dressing. It is another "superherb."

5. LEMONGRASS *(Cymbopogon)*:

Lemongrass has been used in ancient Asian cultures as a fever reducer, immune booster, and flavoring for many dishes. The essential oil made from the plant is also extensively used in Ayurvedic medicine

When processing fresh lemongrass leaves, the air gets filled with their amazing lemony fragrance with no chemicals added. Awesome! The health benefits are also amazing, considering that it is simply a tall grass. Lemongrass makes a great stand-alone healthy tea and tastes great in recipes. I like it cooked with chicken, but it adds a soft lemony flavor to any dish.

Lemongrass contains vitamin A, C, and B6. It also contains high amounts of calcium, iron, phosphorus, magnesium, potassium, as well as Omega 3 and 6. Another amazing balancing herb, lemongrass hits all your Life Centers.

GUT:
- Calms stomach acid while protecting the stomach lining.
- Improves digestion.
- Boosts immune system.
- Improves kidney functions.
- Helps regulate cholesterol.

CHEST:
- Aids in respiratory system functions.
- It clears the lungs of toxins.
- Increases blood flow.
- Helps soothe coughs.

HEAD:
- Reduces headache symptoms.
- Aids in the prevention of dementia.
- Improves brain function.
- Releases serotonin (the "happy drug").
- Enhances your mood.
- Improves central nervous system.

Just like so many other herbs, lemongrass is incredibly easy to grow in warm climates and can also be grown indoors in cooler areas.

This short list of amazing balancing herbs is just an example of how these plants improve your body, mind, and life. After some extensive research, I have concluded that herbs are not only excellent balancing plants, but they are needed to reach homeostasis. If you are not getting the benefits from these plants, you are missing a piece of the life puzzle. In the beginning of the Bible, God gives herbs to mankind. God told man, "See, I have given you every herb that yields seed which is on the face of all the earth, and every tree whose fruit yields seed; to you it shall be for food." (Genesis 1:29) How can you argue with that?

I will mention this one more time: Superfood and super diet fads are not the way to maintain a balanced body and a life in pure homeostasis. Changing what you eat (and the way you eat your food) every couple of months only throws your body out of whack. Consuming a variety of fruit, vegetables, and herbs and avoiding synthetic pharmaceuticals and synthetic chemicals in commercially processed and packaged foods will keep your body and mind in top physical shape. Remember you must:

Get your body right
To get your mind right
To keep your life right!

"The secret of my health is applying honey inside and oil outside."
- Democritus (a contemporary of Hippocrates, who lived to the ripe age of 109)

15
MISCELLANEOUS NUTRIENT BLASTS

There are a few items that don't fall into FV&H category, but they are good to have in your diet. They are a little more controversial, and most people either love them or hate them. From my personal experience, these products have amazing health benefits. So, let's delve into some alternative health food products.

APPLE CIDER VINEGAR:

There are very few noticeable nutrients in apple cider vinegar (ACV): about 11 mg of potassium, 1 mg of sodium, and less than 1 mg of sugar per tablespoon. It has zero carbs, protein, or calories. Yet, it has an amazing way of healing people. I guess we can compare it to rain for the plants. Rain basically has zero nutrients in it, however, when it rains, the growth in plants explodes. Like nature, ACV just has its way: when people use it for health benefits, they tend to be healed.

Even though ACV has not really been scientifically proven to have health benefits, you will find thousands of claims of illness cures from using apple cider vinegar on the internet. I take about a tablespoon a day because it makes me feel healthier.

At one time in my life, I had a serious, bleeding hemorrhoid issue. Gross, I know. But here's a crazy fact; it is believed that 50% of Americans over fifty have hemorrhoids, and I believe this is due to our unhealthy lifestyle choices. Now, I can't say with certainty that ACV healed me, however, shortly after beginning to use it, the bleeding stopped and never came back. Nothing else changed in my life when I started using ACV. My diet had improved a lot over the previous year, and I had all but stopped drinking alcohol well before. But something triggered a healing effect within me and, BAM! just like that, my hemorrhoids got better. Was it the ACV or was it simply another example of the placebo effect? (Just so we're clear, I consumed the apple cider vinegar, I did not use it topically.)

Apple cider vinegar has antifungal, antibacterial, and antiviral properties. You could use it as a topical scrub to clean you up, although it could sting or burn a little, so be careful. You can also use it to disinfect surfaces. I have used it to knock down weeds in my garden. However, you should be aware that vinegar is acidic, and it may kill plants you don't want to kill, so use caution when spraying. It can even be used in organic bug sprays. It is amazing stuff.

GUT:
- Promotes and maintains healthy bacteria in your gut.
- Improves liver and kidney functions.
- Increases nutrient absorption.
- Promotes weight loss.

CHEST:
- Regulates blood sugar.
- Helps to maintain a healthy cardiovascular system.
- May reduce risk of heart disease.

HEAD:
- Improves mood.
- May elevate serotonin levels, which promotes happiness.
- Improves cognitive functions.

Apple cider vinegar is not a miracle cure-all formula, but it does seem to have healing powers. To start using ACV, focus on one area of your body that needs healing and see what happens. ACV has a high acid content and can upset your stomach or create heartburn issues, so start slow, with only one teaspoon a day. You should always mix it with water or juice, or you could even cook with it to get your daily dose.

I take a tablespoon in my daily smoothie, and I really miss that vinegary taste when I don't add it. (Even though I don't relish the flavor of vinegar in general.) On days when I don't take it, my body can feel the difference. It may all just be a placebo effect, of course, but I don't mind, it works for me.

When buying ACV, look for all-natural/organic with a label saying, "with the mother." The "mother" is the yeast and bacteria that was used to create the ACV. You are looking for unrefined, unpasteurized, and unfiltered apple cider vinegar. As with most products, once they get refined and pasteurized, they lose many of their benefits. Simply adding a dose of ACV to your diet has the potential to unlock the happiness effect in your life.

HONEY:

If you are looking for an alternative to sugar (as you should be), look no further. Honey is a magical sugar substitute. Honey's health benefits and uses seem to be unlimited, just Google it. Adding it to your diet may increase your level of happiness as it has mine. It is truly an all-natural happiness effect activator.

The use of honey seems to go back to the beginning of the world. There are prehistoric cave drawings that have been found in Valencia, Spain that picture humans harvesting honey. There is also a fossil of a honeybee found in Europe believed to be 35 million years old.

Honey has been used as medicine by most, if not all, cultures. The oldest known use was around 8,000 years ago. The Babylonians, Egyptians, Assyrians, Greeks, and Romans (you know, all the "great civilizations" throughout ancient history) used honey for its healing power. It has been used as a gift to the gods, wedding gifts between nations, as well as a peace offering between rival nomadic tribes.

Everyone has been on the honey bandwagon since Adam and Eve. Many religions viewed honey as a gift from God. It is mentioned 61 times in the Bible. In many cultures, it has been viewed as sacred, so only the ruling elites and the spiritual leaders could have it. In ancient Egypt, it was used as an embalming fluid and has been found in the pharaohs' tombs. There must be something special about honey!

Recent research has started to prove the health benefits of honey: it is an amazing anti-inflammatory, antioxidant, antiviral, and antibacterial agent. Its uses seem to be limitless, and entire books have been written on the subject. I will simply highlight a couple of interesting benefits.

One benefit I recently discovered is that it can support good dental health. The antibacterial agents in honey can reduce the bacteria in your mouth, which will assist in preventing cavities. Moms and dads, you can let your kids have some honey after dinner, as it will clean their mouths with sweetness.

Here is another pretty cool fact: honey has an enzyme that – when combined with salt and a fluid with a high pH value (like sweat and blood) – will turn into a form of hydrogen peroxide. What does hydrogen peroxide do? It sanitizes, sterilizes, and kills bad bacteria. Nature created this healing bond between humans and honey; I believe that honey has been designed to benefit the human body. The ancients knew honey healed wounds, and 21st century science is proving it. When raw honey is put on a cut, the blood and other body fluids mix with the honey, creating a perfect environment for the hydrogen peroxide effect. This sterilizes the wound and starts the healing process. So cool!

I have put honey on cuts to verify its effectiveness, and it almost immediately stops bleeding. If you make a mixture of honey and aloe, rub it on an open wound, and cover it with a bandage, you will stop the bleeding, while providing antibacterial benefits to the area. This can speed up the healing process.

I use honey almost every day in a multitude of ways. I believe it is part of the puzzle of perfect health and balance, as it helps my body and mind reach homeostasis. Honey has over two hundred active micronutrients that benefit your body and mind (see Abdulwahid Ajibola, Joseph P. Chamunorwa, and Kennedy H. Erlwanger's article entitled "Nutraceutical values of natural honey and its contribution to human health and wealth" published in 2012 in *Nutrition & Metabolism*).

Honey is a superfood. Nature makes it with zero help from humans. I like to think of it as a gift from nature, or God if you prefer. Let's look at the three Life Centers and see how honey can help you reach homeostasis.

GUT:
- Improves digestion.
- Promotes good bacteria growth in your gut.
- May prevent liver and kidney damage.
- Has prebiotic properties.
- Boosts immune system.

CHEST:
- Reduces risk of heart disease.
- Improves blood flow.
- Reduces coughs and sore throats.
- Improves respiratory system functions.

HEAD:
- Improves memory.
- Improves cognitive functions.
- Improves brain development.
- Reduces stress.
- Improves sleep.
- Assists in the development of your central nervous system.

There are a few things that you should be aware of, though. First, most of the honey you can buy in the store has been heated, refined, pasteurized, and filtered. As raw honey may contain a form of bacteria that causes botulism, a paralyzing disease, the FDA recommends pasteurization, or high-heat treatment to kill the bacteria spores. (Because of the possible presence of these bacterial organisms, it is highly recommended that honey should not be given to children under the age of one.) However, the pasteurization and filtration process also kills most of the nutrients the bees worked so hard to gather for you. When you buy honey, always try to buy raw, unfiltered, unpasteurized honey. It is the way nature makes it, and nature is a professional at providing everything we need without our help.

Honey Hack: Once you heat honey to 98 degrees, you begin killing many of the nutrients. If you want to cook with honey and have all the amazing benefits, let your concoction cool down and add the honey at the end of your cooking process.

One of several controversial issues with honey is its use for allergy prevention. The theory is that because bees collect an assortment of pollen, if you eat local honey, it will raise your immunity to local pollen. The problem with this theory is that bees collect pollen from flowers, and most of your allergies are reactions to grass and tree pollen, rather than flowers. Nevertheless, many people swear by honey's ability to fight allergies so maybe there is some truth in it. However, it may also simply be the placebo effect again. But if it works for you, just continue its use.

Today, honey is the center of a moral controversy. Is it an ethical thing to take – steal? – honey from the bees? Great question! Nature provides for our abundance, and bees as well as their honey are a part of nature, as are we. So maybe, just maybe, the bees are grateful that we enjoy the health benefits they provide for us through honey.

Every single beekeeper I know loves their bees and would do whatever they can to ensure they have a fantastic life. The concern is that commercial breeders take all the bees' honey and then feed them sugar water through winter. Yes, it happens. However, the sugar water helps the bees start making honey again so that they will have plenty of food stored for winter. If beekeepers were stealing food from the mouths of bees, we wouldn't have any honey, oranges, or avocados, and the beekeeper would not have any bees to make money from.

Also, many people are bothered by the fact that honey is not vegan. Well, honey is made from plants, so it is, in a sense, vegan. In my opinion, eating honey is not less ethical than eating fruit and veggies, as plants are alive as well! Plants communicate with each other, they feel pain and stress, and yet, we rip them out of the ground and gorge ourselves on them without a second thought. That concept may be a bit of a stretch for many of you, but please keep an open mind and keep reading as we'll talk about this in a future chapter.

Another argument that people often mention is that bees make honey for bees. Well, fruit is also produced by plants to propagate more of that plant; an animal takes the fruit, discards the seed, and hopefully, the seed will sprout, thus ensuring the species' survival. Technically, when you pick fruit, you are stopping that plant from creating new life. The same goes for taking maple syrup – the syrup is there for the tree, yet, we take it for our own use.

The last argument I'll address is that we're killing the bees, causing colony collapse and creating disease. Well, many studies indicate that much of the colony collapse and disease is created by man-made chemicals found in fertilizers, herbicides, and pesticides, and quite possibly **GMO** crops themselves. The chemicals destroying bees are the ones that are used to grow many of the (vegan!) fruits and vegetables. Just saying.

My feelings are that forty thousand years of documented medicinal and nutritional use overrules forty years of vegan idealism, even though I believe that the vegan lifestyle is extremely beneficial for our health. I eat mostly fruit and vegetables because they are life-giving, but so is honey. So, go out and buy some raw, unfiltered, locally grown honey and enjoy this natural gift from bees without any guilt.

SECTION 5

CANNABIS & HEMP

"We created the war on drugs to criminalize black people and the antiwar left." - John Ehrlichman (White House Domestic Affairs Advisor under President Nixon)

16
THE GREAT CANNABIS CONSPIRACY

By now, I have given you a basic starting point to create a lasting happiness effect by embracing nature in your food and medicine. I highly recommend that you dive deeper into the research of plants as food and medicine for yourself. Get educated; the feeling of knowing things is empowering.

I cannot talk about natural health and happiness without discussing cannabis and hemp. I feel it is important to speak out and share the truth about a plant that has never killed anyone and provides numerous health benefits. It's a plant that has been used by governments throughout history to control populations and destroy lives. But it's also a plant that heals; a plant that I credit with saving my life from opioid death.

For many years, I would abuse my prescriptions, and as I ran out of medicine, withdrawal symptoms took over – stomach cramps, vomiting, diarrhea, and a general feeling of misery. However, cannabis would calm me down and help take my mind away from my pain. Growing cannabis gave me a reason to wake up every day. I believed that my plants would help me, so I had to ensure they grew well. If my plants failed, I would fail. Yes, I could have bought marijuana on the street or at a legal dispensary, however black-market dealers are not always reliable, and purchasing from legal dispensaries is very expensive with no help from insurance. Growing my own supply seemed to be the best solution.

Cannabis is a misunderstood plant, so now I want you to have a basic understanding of what cannabis is and how it can benefit our bodies. There is much more to learn; science has barely scratched the surface. Hopefully, with the simple facts that I provide, you will understand that cannabis is a life-giving plant, not the demon weed we have been told about. It is also not simply a party drug, although that is how it is primarily being used today. To know the whole story, please go online and learn all you can about its history and the health benefits. It's fascinating!

Marijuana (cannabis) and hemp are in the same plant family, *Cannabis sativa*. However, there are a few distinct differences. Hemp has almost no THC (the chemical that creates the high feeling) compared to cannabis, and cannabis is the more medicinal variety of the genus – just like holy basil is more medicinal than other varieties of basil.

Both marijuana and hemp have been used for centuries. Archeologists have found the cannabis plant material in a medicine bag buried with a shaman dating over 2,500 years ago. Hemp has also been used for thousands of years. During the 1700s, American farmers were required to dedicate at least one acre of farmland to growing hemp due to its many uses. Hemp is also beneficial for the soil, as it removes toxins from farmland while returning good nutrients into the ground. As it can heal the soil, it's often referred to as a "phytoremediation" plant.

Unfortunately, the plant has also been used as a political tool to control the masses with examples dating back to the 1300s. Let me give you one example. In America during the 1930s, Mexican immigrants and African Americans were considered a threat to white society. They were also associated with smoking marijuana, which is similar in appearance and genetic makeup to hemp. The conspiracy theory is that around this time, hemp was just about to make a big financial splash in the oil, fabric, and paper industries, as well as other commercial markets due to a new and less expensive processing method. The lumber industry, in which the Hearst family-owned billions of dollars, and the chemical business run by the DuPont family, along with Andrew Mellon (the nation's wealthiest man) had concerns that this new processing method would severely cut into the monopolies they held. The leaders of these large conglomerates got together and decided to raise the public's fear of marijuana and hemp as well as breed public fear of immigrants and minorities. You know, kill two birds with one stone.

As Randolph Hearst owned several newspapers, it was easy for these conglomerates to run anti-cannabis propaganda campaigns. The media was soon full of fake stories on the horrors of marijuana. The businesses also used their power and influence to have a family relative of Mellon – a guy named Harry Anslinger – nominated as the founding commissioner of the Federal Bureau of Narcotics in 1930. (It sounds like a real Monsanto/Bayer move, doesn't it?) Soon after this, cannabis was deemed illegal and the rest, as they say, is history.

People had been receiving the benefits of hemp since the beginning of time. Taking it out of our diets has removed vital nutrients and has had negative consequences on our health. Shortly after cannabis prohibition, cancer rates went up, and cases of diabetes, poor blood circulation, chronic inflammation started to rise. Could there be a connection?

Throughout the history of the world, hemp had been required to be grown for its value. Ship sails and clothes were made from the fabric. Also, you could burn the oil, you could use it as medicine, and you could consume it. It was also used as livestock feed: all the amazing nutrients and cannabinoids (we'll get to that in just a minute) were fed to the livestock that everyone ate. Therefore, we were all eating CBD and hundreds of other beneficial nutrients every time we ate meat. Today, our meat comes from livestock that was fed mostly GMO corn and is potentially filled with chemical fertilizers, pesticides, herbicides, antibiotics, and hormones. YUCK!

Here is a comparison of corn and hemp seed nutritional values*:

	Corn	Hemp seed
Calories	177	111
Fiber	4.6 g	2 g
Protein	5.4 g	6.3 g
Fat	7.9 g	9 g
Carbs	41 g	2.6 g
Sodium	8.2 mg	0
Potassium	205 mg	240 mg
Magnesium	211 mg	140 mg
Phosphorous	349 mg	330 mg
Zinc	1.1 mg	1.9 mg
Iron	4.5 mg	1.6 mg
Vitamins	A, B-6, C, K	A, B-1,3,6, C, D, E, K

*Data taken from various online sources. Values are for hemp seeds. The whole cannabis plant would have additional nutrients, but currently the statistics are not verifiable. According to some studies, cannabis contains the perfect 3-1-1 ratio of Omega 3, 6, and 9, which is the optimum for human health. Cannabis also has a variety of terpenes, micronutrients, phytonutrients, and over 100 cannabinoids that interact with our bodies.

I hope you realize that American politicians and corporate interests have lied to us to ensure profits and maintain control. Most of the world has prohibited cannabis use based on pressure from the United States. Countries that belong to the United Nations have all signed the Single Convention on Narcotic Drugs of 1961, which prohibits marijuana use based on the false assumption that it is harmful.

With new laws passed every year, cannabis legislation is changing, along with the mainstream attitude. My hope is that one day, cannabis and hemp will be used to benefit humanity legally, and it will not be used to control people or just to get people high. Cannabis and hemp contain a plethora of nutrients, and they assist in balancing the body. To me, it simply makes sense to have them as part of our diets.

Now you know how cannabis and hemp became illegal, it is time to educate you on how they can heal you. You are probably wondering how they work with our body. It is amazing, and science has just begun to discover it. This is an extremely exciting time for hemp and cannabis research. Turn the page and you will find out.

"I have found in my study that cannabis is a really safe, effective and non-toxic alternative to many standard medicines." - Phillip Denney, MD

17
CANNABINOIDS AND YOUR ENDOCANNABINOID SYSTEM

What are cannabinoids, and where can we find them? Do we need cannabinoids? What is the endocannabinoid system (ECS)? Can cannabis trigger the happiness effect without making us high?

Even with over ten years of self-education, I still don't understand the topic fully, and neither do scientists. It was illegal to research cannabis for the past eighty years, so there is a lot of catching up to do. The science is complex, so this book will only give you some basics that will hopefully demonstrate why cannabis and hemp should be included in your war chest for health and happiness. Hold on to your seat because you might get blown away.

The endocannabinoid system (ECS) is a complex system that follows a similar path in your body as your central nervous system. That's right – the ECS touches almost every part of your body. It seems odd that a system that has a connection to everything in your body was only discovered in 1992. And it was only discovered because two scientists in Israel, Dr. Lumir Hanus and Dr. William Devane, were trying to understand why cannabis has so many positive attributes while having very few, if any, negative side effects.

All vertebrates have an endocannabinoid system. This system is responsible for regulating nearly every vital bodily function, so it ensures that your body can maintain homeostasis. In simple terms, a cannabinoid is a chemical compound that acts on your cannabinoid receptors, which make up the ECS. We already know from research that there are at least two cannabinoid receptors (CB1 & CB2), which react to cannabinoids. The CB1 receptors are found mainly in the brain, lungs, liver, and kidneys (all three Life Centers!), and they also follow your central nervous system. The CB2 receptors are found in your blood and bones.

Visualize the CB1 and CB2 receptors as nerve endings. They are everywhere in your body, interacting with every part of you. These receptors receive cannabinoids and put them to work in your body.

There are over one hundred known cannabinoids in the cannabis plant including THC and CBD. Cannabinoids mediate communication between cells, thus these chemicals contribute to your body's overall health. Without cannabinoids, neither your endocannabinoid system nor your body would ever be in complete balance.

But you have been told your whole life that marijuana makes you dumb. First, there are no successful studies proving that cannabis kills brain cells. In fact, it has been found to increase and support brain cell activity. It has been successfully studied for its ability to reduce and prevent some symptoms of Alzheimer's disease and dementia. The "dumb and lazy" stereotype comes from the media and misconstrued social norms. I know many cannabis consumers who are athletes, lawyers, doctors, and business owners. They are the exact opposite of dumb and lazy. Michael Phelps, the 23-time Olympic gold medal winner admitted to consuming cannabis. I believe that winning 23 gold medals kind of validates the potential of cannabis as a health supplement.

When I medicate with marijuana, I can feel my body and mind relax. Because of this relaxed state, I must stay focused, or my mind will wander. A drifting mind is great for creativity, but not so much for driving. I highly recommend not driving if you are not accustomed to the mind amending effects of cannabis.

When smoked, cannabis provides medicinal benefits: it helps you to relax (think Prozac), it reduces phlegm in amyotrophic lateral sclerosis (ALS) patients and has been researched for increasing your airway and lung capacity. It has *not* been linked to lung cancer. It may even alleviate many asthma symptoms. In my opinion, cannabis and hemp are super plants.

That's all great, but you just don't want to *feel high*. When consumed raw, cannabis will NOT make you high – it might be better for you than kale, and you already know that kale is awesome. For marijuana to get you high, it must be heated to over 215 degrees. When the plant material is heated, a chemical reaction occurs, turning THCA and CBDA, into THC and CBD. Only then will you get the high, dizzy feeling associated with smoking marijuana.

Uncooked and unprocessed marijuana will provide you with vitamins, minerals, micronutrients, terpenes, cannabinoids, phytocannabinoids, phytonutrients, and more. A simple method of consumption is to infuse coconut oil with raw cannabis. I usually soak the plant material (flowers, leaves, stems) in coconut oil for 30 days then cook the concoction for 2–4 hours at 160 degrees, ensuring the temperature never reaches 200 degrees. I can then add it to a smoothie or simply take a spoonful to receive all the nutrients that cannabis contains, without getting "high." (If you want the "high," you could cook the oil at 220 for the same amount of time. This activates the THC, which could then make you feel high.)

Now you are probably wondering where the body gets the cannabinoids that activate the endocannabinoid system, since marijuana has been illegal. The simple answer is that there are other plants that can simulate or mimic cannabinoids: recently discovered phytocannabinoids and cannabimimetic compounds can react with both CB1 and CB2 receptors. (A phytocannabinoid is any plant-derived natural product capable of either directly interacting with cannabinoid receptors or sharing a chemical similarity with cannabinoids or both. A cannabimimetic is any substance with similar or "mimicking" pharmacological effects to those of cannabis.)

Some of the other foods that can stimulate your CB receptors are:

- BLACK PEPPER: Science has started to prove that black pepper is great for you. It assists your body in absorbing nutrients, and it also reacts with your body's ECS.
- CLOVE: It can mimic cannabis and react with your CB receptors.
- SUNFLOWER: The *Helichrysum* variety and sunflower lecithin help your body to absorb nutrients more efficiently and may react with CB receptors.
- ECHINACEA: It has a cannabinoid that reacts with your CB2 receptor and helps strengthen the immune system and reduce inflammation and pain. Echinacea also makes a great tea for colds and coughs.
- FLAX SEED: Surprisingly, it has CBD and some other cannabinoids, but it is not as highly concentrated as cannabis. So, until marijuana is legal, you can eat a boatload of flax seeds for your CBD needs.
- CHOCOLATE: Chocolate (preferably dark) also reacts with your ECS, and it also helps you to relax. However, the refined sugar in artificial chocolate makes it hard for you to relax.
- HOPS: Yes, the stuff you make beer with has some minor cannabinoids. No wonder beer makes you happy.
- BLACK TRUFFLES: They contain anandamide, a chemical that reacts with your ECS in a way similar to cannabis. It makes you feel happy.

You can see that there are several plants that can interact with your ECS, however, the cannabinoids in cannabis specifically target the ECS, while other plants only try to adapt to or mimic it. Which one do you think will work better with your body? A plant specifically designed by nature for your body or a plant that must change to work with your body? To me, the answer seems obvious.

"CBD helps with pain, stress and anxiety. It has the benefits of marijuana without the high." - Jennifer Aniston

18
CBD FACTS

First off, I know from hundreds of testimonials that CBD alone helps many people heal from different ailments. Even though some of the healing might only happen thanks to the placebo effect, CBD is quickly becoming a major superfood, super diet, and super drug. But there are a couple issues that you should be aware of.

My first concern is that the media is only promoting a ridiculously small piece of the cannabis puzzle. CBD is a newly found compound in the cannabis plant that has not yet been completely studied or understood. It is only one of hundreds of cannabinoids, vitamins, minerals, micronutrients, phytonutrients, and fiber that cannabis contains. If you are taking only CBD, you are missing out on most of the plant's benefits.

When buying your CBD products, you should understand that hemp seed oil contains about 1/100th of the benefits that the whole plant contains. Seeds are just not a great source of nutrients. Hemp seed oil is about as beneficial for you as olive or coconut oil. When purchasing CBD in oils or lotions, you want to look for the following terms: "entourage effect," "full spectrum," or "whole plant." These are the phrases that are used to describe when the entire plant was used in the processing of the oil. If the label only says "hemp seed," walk away. Only the whole plant will allow your body to reach homeostasis. (Also, if you are looking for pain relief, or I should say, more immediate pain relief, you really do need the THC as well.)

Another thing to look for is the type of carrier oil used for the CBD product. The carrier oil will have a lot to do with the final health benefits. It could be any oil such as coconut, olive, grapeseed, or MCT (multi-chain triglycerides). Cannabis nutrients like to attach to the fat cells in oil, so the higher the fat content, the better the extraction. I personally feel raw, organic, unfiltered coconut oil is the best oil to use when extracting cannabis due to its high nutrient values and fat content.

Many people are concerned with the total milligrams of CBD per serving (and per package). I want this to be perfectly clear and simple for you: There are about a dozen ways of calculating the milligrams, as there are no set standards. Every company calculates this number a little differently, and there is little verification of what the companies are claiming.

Besides, most companies test ten percent or less of the entire crop that was used to make the oil. Every seed produces a slightly different plant (just as every human is slightly different). Therefore, when they figure out the dosage, the numbers may not be completely accurate. Until we get some more in-depth knowledge, it's simply better to forget about the milligrams! There is some research that states an average adult would probably benefit most from approximately fifteen milligrams a day. However, this is not a scientific fact. And as already stated, we are all different with different needs.

CBD alone will not make you high; it most likely won't give you any immediate feelings. Remember what I have said about nature: It takes time. CBD will improve how your body works, but it takes a little bit of time for your body to absorb and begin using the nutrients effectively. You won't notice how good you feel right away.

Today, cannabis is a new fad, and the price is ridiculous – it costs the same as saffron, the world's most expensive spice. Saffron is an anti-inflammatory, antidepressant, antioxidant, and it has cancer-fighting properties. It is incredibly difficult to grow, harvest, and process. It takes around five thousand flowers to produce one ounce of the spice, and it takes around twelve hours to pick five thousand flowers, as they must be harvested by hand. All in all, it takes about ten times more work growing saffron than it does growing and processing hemp. The price of saffron is around forty dollars an ounce – just like cannabis oil! The two plants have similar benefits (except for cannabinoids), so why are they the same price per ounce?

Olive and coconut oil – which are also extremely healthy for you – are much more time-intensive to produce than hemp, and yet the oil is about one tenth the cost. Coconut oil costs around fifty cents per ounce. Cannabis-infused coconut oil shouldn't cost more than a dollar an ounce, but it costs around forty times that much, because it could make you high. Hopefully, once America legalizes the plant for everyone, the price will reflect the amount of work it takes to produce. The sooner we remove the legal over-regulation of the plant, the sooner the price will fall so that everyone can benefit from the plant.

If you are thinking about medicating with cannabis or hemp, to start I would recommend one full eyedropper (about one milliliter) of cannabis oil twice a day (where it's legal). If it is not legal, I recommend whole-plant CBD oil made with coconut, grapeseed, hemp, or some other natural oil.

After two weeks, evaluate how you feel. Has anything changed? If nothing has changed, add a third dose, and wait two more weeks. After about a month, you should be able to cut down to one dose a day. As the nutrients are already in your system, now you just need a maintenance dose every couple of days.

Within thirty days, you should be feeling more complete, more balanced, and happier. Your body should begin to function better, and you should be moving around more easily, because your body is reaching homeostasis. Cannabis and hemp are two all-natural plants that can release the happiness effect all by themselves. What could be easier than adding a plant to your diet to change for the better? I know that it improves my body, and it helps trigger my happiness effect. But I also know that consuming cannabis will not feel right to everyone and that's okay. It may require you to have an open mind, and my suggestion would be to give it a try before making a final judgment.

SECTION 6

MOVEMENT OUTDOORS

"If we could give every individual the right amount of nourishment and exercise, not too little and not too much, we would have found the safest way to health." - Hippocrates

19
YOUR BODY NEEDS MOVEMENT

Our bodies are designed to be in motion. If you are just sitting around watching TV, letting life go by, you are slowly killing yourself. Sitting still for long periods of time will allow your cells to get lazy. Your muscles will stop functioning well, your heart loses strength, thus altering your blood pressure to unsafe levels, and your lungs will not process oxygen as efficiently. Your stomach won't process food too well, which causes your liver and kidneys to stop processing toxins. When you're not moving around, you are throwing all three Life Centers off balance in a monumental way. Not moving destroys your entire body and mind.

As my opioid addiction spiraled out of control, it was not uncommon for me to sit and watch television and play video games for eight to twelve hours a day. I had been an active guy, coaching my kids' athletics as well as playing slow-pitch softball. But the more I sat around, the less my body wanted to move. The less I moved, the less my mind wanted to work. Lethargy became my norm. Bad food, prescription drugs, and sitting inside all day was killing me. I looked unhealthy, and I felt unhealthy. However, as my transformation began, and I was feeling better and thinking more clearly, exercise was another necessary step in my journey. Once I began moving again, my body knew it needed more, and my mind started pushing me to go outside and do something physical.

Physical activity increases blood circulation, which brings fresh blood to replace the old, "tired" blood. It also gets your lungs moving, bringing you fresh oxygen to help build new cells. Your muscles and ligaments were designed for movement. When they don't get used, they will stop working altogether.

Exercising or moving your body around also makes your skin healthier. As fresh blood is sent to your skin, it refreshes and heals it. When your skin is healthy and balanced, guess what? You can spend more time outside catching some vitamin D from the sun. Your skin is the first line of defense against germs, so you are creating a strong immune system simply by moving around.

Living things are always growing, the universe is ever expanding. Everything in our world is always in motion. This is the "law of rhythm," which states that life is always moving like an ocean tide. The fact that everything must move in the universe seems to be telling us that we need to be in motion as well.

All of us need to exercise, or at least spend some time throughout your day moving. Feel free to choose the type of exercise or activity you enjoy the most. I have never enjoyed simply exercising or lifting weights, but I do love playing team sports, cycling, and gardening. (In Chapter 21, you will learn how working in a garden can be extremely therapeutic and healthy for you.) The benefits that you get from physical activity will positively affect all three Life Centers. Making movement a priority is imperative if you plan to experience the happiness effect.

Getting outside and walking is an easy way to get some exercise while also embracing your community and keeping up on current events. I walk an average of five thousand steps – a little over two miles – a day according to my smartphone. I suggest that you also use your phone – or some other device – to track your daily activity, as this really helps to keep you informed of how much you move throughout your day. If you walk under five thousand steps, it might be a good idea for you to get outside and walk some more.

Remember, life is about balance. You don't necessarily need a one-hour workout every day. Most of us do not need the high-octane workout that professional athletes do. But I'll let you in on a secret: once you begin moving or exercising, your body will want more. Who knows? In a year, you may be the one leading the high-performance workout!

You should get outside and move around for at least one hour a day if you can. If you can spend three or more hours a day outside, you will see an even more dramatic improvement in how your body and mind function. It is okay if you don't have a whole hour at a time to dedicate to exercise outdoors; try to take fifteen minutes and do some walking outside three or four times a day. It is not a lot of time, but it will benefit you as well as give you your daily dose of vitamin D.

"The art of healing comes from nature, not from the physician."
- Paracelsus, a 16th-century German-Swiss physician

20
NATURE THERAPY

The next secret I will share with you is that you must embrace your connection to nature. I believe it is important to genuinely feel our connection with the natural universe. When looking to connect with nature, try to really *feel* the experience; listen to the sounds, breathe deeply, and notice the variety of smells in the air. Observe the plants, as well as the wildlife, bugs, bees, and the animals. If you live in a city, just sit near two or three small plants and simply enjoy their presence. Look at them, see the detail in their leaves, pay attention to how they grow, and don't feel silly for talking to them.

I garden on a 16-by-16-foot patio, small by most standards. However, I am deeply connected to my plants. I look forward to seeing them every day. I check on them daily to ensure their life is going along smoothly. In return, they give me joy. They provide nutrients and flowers to appreciate, as well as nectar for pollinators.

I spend at least an hour a day outside (usually four or more). I'm either sitting or working in my garden (I could spend all day working with my plants), visiting public gardens and parks, walking along the beach, or just watching nature happen around me. I prefer to be outside, rain or shine. The feeling of joy that surrounds you when in nature is extremely therapeutic.

There is a growing trend in Japan called "shinrin-yoku" or "forest bathing." People go into nature and immerse themselves in their surroundings by listening to the sounds, feeling the breeze, enjoying the smells, and simply getting in touch with and appreciating nature. I can't wait to experience this when I get to Japan.

Why would you want to sit in a big field or be covered by a dense forest canopy? Because studies show that interacting with nature can heal your body and mind. Simply by being in nature without any other effort, you are creating a healthy, balanced body. You are invoking the happiness effect. You are a part of nature, so it will make sense when I tell you that nature blasts your three Life Centers with health benefits. All you must do is go outside and embrace a tree. Check out what nature can do for your Life Centers:

GUT:
- Improves liver functions.
- Improves kidney functions.
- Improves digestion.
- Strengthens the immune system.

CHEST:
- Lowers blood pressure.
- Improves blood quality.
- Improves lung functions.

HEAD:
- Reduces stress.
- Reduces depression.
- Improves focus.
- Improves cognitive functions.

Phytoncides are chemicals that plants use to fight off disease and pests, and they also release them into the atmosphere, which help improve our immune system. When we breathe them in, they respond to our bodies by increasing the number and activity of a certain type of white blood cell that scientists call "natural killer" cells. These white blood cells fight back against tumors and cancer cells in your body. Plants have been designed to heal you just by being around them. How crazy is that?

Nature has been designed to assist us in healing our bodies and minds, but we have cut ourselves off from a free source of medical care by moving to cities and surrounding ourselves with concrete and steel. We have taken our free universal healthcare system and cut it down. What once was our way of life is no longer normal to us. But your body, which has evolved over millions of years, is still craving a connection to nature.

Did you know that within ten minutes of being surrounded by nature, your body starts to benefit? As your blood pressure is lowered and highly oxygenated blood reaches your brain, you begin to feel happy and content. The more you relax, the healthier your body is getting. After spending just three days immersed in nature, the calming and healing benefits stay with you for over thirty days! So, when you plan that weekend getaway to the lake, you are planning a health session. Your insurance company should pick up part of the tab! A trip to nature has the potential to make you healthier than the pharmaceutical chemicals your insurance pays for.

Did you know that sticking your hands in soil is healthy? Yes, it is. Your parents yelling at you to stop playing in the dirt was actually a bad thing. Eating (I don't eat or recommend eating dirt, but there are people who do it!) and playing in dirt, especially as a child, stimulates the immune system. By stimulating your immune system in small doses, you are making your body stronger and less susceptible to disease. Pharmaceutical companies do the same thing when they make vaccines: they stimulate your immune system by giving it a small piece of disease. Why not just get in the dirt and get vaccinated naturally? You now have a great excuse to get dirty. "It's healthcare, Mom and Dad."

I tell people that I am fearless in the face of colds. When they ask how I can be so confident, I show them my fingernails which frequently still have a little soil in them from gardening. Ask my parents and they will tell you that when I was a child, I could be placed in a sterile environment, left for an hour, and I would come out covered in dirt.

Playing in the dirt is also therapeutic; it may play a role in lifting depression. *Live Science* published a study in 2007 that showed that "exposure to friendly soil bacteria microbes could improve your mood by boosting the immune system just as effectively as some pharmaceutical drugs." Those friendly soil microbes are called *Mycobacterium vaccae*. It appears that these little organisms trigger our happy centers.

Everything in this entire universe was designed to work together. We are all connected. When we fight against nature by destroying forests and spraying chemicals on our farmland, we create cancers, both in ourselves and in the world. But if we let nature work its magic, we will all benefit – you, me, humanity, and the planet. We will be in perfect homeostasis.

"Flowers always make people better, happier, and more helpful; they are sunshine, food and medicine for the soul." - Luther Burbank

21
GARDEN THERAPY

Now you know how nature was designed to heal us and assist us in our search for the happiness effect and creating a healthy, balanced, happy, and abundant life. But what if you cannot get into nature? The answer is that you must create your own natural environment. Create a garden for your health. Gardening will enhance your three Life Centers just as effectively as being in a forest.

Even two or three potted plants on a balcony or a window ledge can heal you both mentally and physically. Studies have shown that patients in hospital recover on average one full day faster when allowed to enjoy a garden setting versus those patients who stayed in their rooms. This healing effect was noticeable even when the patients only had a view of nature versus looking at a wall. The studies do not say, but I'm certain that the patients who were let outside also felt happier as they healed, because nature activates the happiness effect. We should ask the nurses which patients were more enjoyable to work with.

When you are in a garden, you are healing your body and mind. First, being outside in the sun for fifteen minutes will give you all the vitamin D your body needs for the day. Vitamin D is needed to help your body absorb nutrients like phosphorus and calcium, which makes your bones strong. Vitamin D also keeps your immune system functioning at a high level. Working in the garden is also a form of exercise: gardening gets your body moving, which improves all three

Life Centers while strengthening the immune system. What a simple and effective way to stay happy, stress free, and healthy!

Gardening also helps you to create a healthy bond with nature. It forces you to become responsible for another life. Yes, I believe that plants are not simply alive, but they also seem to have feelings. In his – somewhat controversial – study, Grover Cleveland Backster Jr. used sophisticated polygraph equipment to show that plants changed their electrical vibrations whenever they were damaged. The plants appeared to be able to discern the intent of the person who approached them and could even remember past bad experiences with people. The studies were never consistently duplicated, however, from my personal experience, plants seem to grow better and fight off pests and disease faster when I focus on them every day. Could it be that they are responding to my vibrations of love and care? Or do I just stay on top of garden maintenance more efficiently, so the plants simply grow better? I think a little bit of both.

I have a star fruit (carambola) tree that I started from a seed of a store-bought fruit. It was growing in a five-gallon bucket, and I was immensely proud of it. After about three years of growth, I wanted to harvest fruit, but the tree was never blooming. I was getting extremely frustrated. I did some research on the different varieties of carambola, and I found a "dwarf" variety that would provide fruit in only one year. I must tell you that I never used to really talk to my plants (although now I talk to all of them), but I said to my tree, "If I don't see some fruit soon, I will have to replace you with a dwarf tree." About six days later, the tree began to bloom, and within a month she had almost fifty baby star fruits on her skinny limbs! Sadly, I ended up harvesting only five fruits, as the rest were either blown off in storms or eaten by birds. However, it was still a very cool experience. Did all this happen because I threatened the tree? We may never know, but it is an interesting coincidence.

Over time you will begin to realize that your plants respond to your positive actions, the same as people will. The minute you plant a seed, you develop a connection to the plant. Just like a baby, your new plant needs you to guide it until it can survive on its own. If you give them nourishment and love while they are young, they will give back in abundance when they are fully grown. This simple process of nurturing plants greatly benefits your mental health. It makes you feel alive and full of purpose. It gives you a reason to wake up every day. Even on bad days when the world is crashing down on you, the minute you walk into your garden, the challenges and stress of life seem to evaporate. It helps you to create the happiness effect without much effort. Watching a life that you helped create is a magical experience.

Garden hack: Always pick your fruit and vegetables in the morning. They seem to have more flavor than food harvested later in the day. I have my own theories why this is so, and maybe in my next book, I'll fill you in on the secret. Stay tuned.

Growing your own fruit, vegetables, and herbs is very fulfilling. I can think of few things that I like better than picking a tomato, strawberry, or apple off the plant and eating it. They simply taste better when they are home-grown. You also get the awesome feeling of accomplishment, which brings with it an abundance of happy feelings. I almost always have more food than I can eat from the plants that I have grown. Sharing my abundance seems to be part of the good feeling I get from gardening. When you give freely, you will always get back in abundance. Sharing, especially sharing something that is special to you, automatically triggers the happiness effect, making it another super easy trick to maintain positivity in your life. As I continually say, the universe is designed for our abundance.

"Sorry, there's no magic bullet. You gotta eat healthy and live healthy to be healthy and look healthy. End of story." - Morgan Spurlock

22
A QUICK REVIEW

Let's do a quick review of what we have covered this far on our journey together. Soon we will be discussing how to improve your mindset, and I simply want to reinforce what you have learned thus far before moving on. You should be proud of yourself for sticking around and following through with improving your life. You are a searcher of truth, and you have learned how to improve your health naturally. You have learned the importance of embracing nature every day. You are now more educated on how to create the happiness effect physically, and after you complete reading the next sections, you will know how to become totally balanced by creating the happiness effect mentally.

We have learned about how processed food and synthetic medicine are killing us slowly. You should now understand that our food and drugs are predominantly controlled by only a couple of companies, whose agenda is not necessarily our good health, but a healthy profit. When taking synthetic prescription drugs, you are altering your body unnaturally, which will create other health issues requiring more synthetic drugs (remember, great business model!). Your body is designed to process natural foods in a way that benefits your three Life Centers. Eating and medicating naturally creates few, if any, unwanted and unnatural side effects.

When your body is balanced by nature, you will be able to see life in a more positive way. You will be able to maintain your positive momentum, which will create more abundance for you. During my forty years of unhealthy living, I was an extremely negative person. I disliked or distrusted most people. I saw most events in my life as negative. However, as my body began getting natural nutrients, and I removed synthetic drugs from my life, things started looking up, and they will for you as well. I began seeing things more positively. My finances did not change, my job, which I loathed, didn't change; the only thing in my life that had changed was my diet, and this began triggering the happiness effect in me without any other external reasons. This will happen for you as well.

We have learned how our body has three Life Centers: the gut, the chest, and the head. Most fruit, vegetables, and herbs affect these areas in a positive way. Honey and apple cider vinegar can also help to balance these three essential areas of your body. Maintaining your Life Centers in a natural way will create homeostasis in your life. Remember my creed:

You must get your body right
To get your mind right
To get your life right.

Every plant and concoction we have discussed has anti-cancer properties. Many of the foods mentioned are being studied not only for their prevention abilities, but also for their curing effects. If you consume a variety of fruit, vegetables, and herbs every day, you will greatly reduce the risk of many other health issues, including colds, brain fog, depression and more. The key, as I have stated throughout this book, is balance.

You are part of nature, so it only makes sense that you must interact with nature to reach a balanced, happy life. By stepping outside, your body begins to heal without any work on your part. You may remember that plants release chemicals (phytoncides) that react with our body and mind, helping us become healthier and happier. After ten minutes in nature, you begin to receive the healing benefits that plants provide – these benefits include reducing depression and anxiety and improving blood circulation as well as your cardiovascular and digestive systems. You simply must walk outside and breathe.

Health hack: Try to always breathe through your nose. Nose breathing is proven to improve every area of your body. The three Life Centers all get a boost from it. Mouth breathing was only designed as a backup plan.

If you cannot get into a forest or park, you can still get connected to nature by creating a garden. Even caring for one or two plants can give your life purpose as well as help you to stay healthy and happy. Even if you accidentally kill a plant (it happens to all of us, no worries), don't give up! When you do get flowers or can harvest the food, it will create an amazing feeling of confidence, pride, and a sense of accomplishment.

Now that I have shown you how fruit, vegetables, herbs, honey, apple cider vinegar, cannabis, gardening, and simply walking outside will make you healthier and happier, I believe you are ready for the final secrets of life: positivity and gratitude. Together with nature, these two life principles will enable you to automatically create and maintain the happiness effect in your life.

Turn the page...

SECTION 7

POSITIVE THOUGHTS

"We are what we think. All that we are arises with our thoughts. With our thoughts, we make the world." - Buddha

23
YOU CONTROL HOW YOU FEEL

Everything always works out. You are here, you are alive, you are reading this book. If today is bad, wait until tomorrow, because tomorrow could be your best day ever. Things are guaranteed to change. You may be facing some major challenges in your life right now. We all do from time to time. However, if you stay positive, look for the good, and be patient, your challenges will turn into accomplishments.

Knowing that our lives are constantly changing is a very cool thing. You can use this knowledge to control how changes affect your life. Even unwanted, forced change can be used to create your own happiness effect. Frequently I will have my day planned out. When I wake up, I try to set an intention for what I want to accomplish and how I want my day to go. But as it is with life, my plans, like yours, can quickly go astray. For example, I sometimes write at a small table right outside my door. It seems that as soon as I get into the groove, my dog decides he wants to come outside and play. I'm right in the middle of a powerful thought, and he keeps jumping at the door. Now I have a choice: I can let this make me upset and ruin my day, or I can accept it and use it to my advantage.

After what can seem like hours, I realize that I need to take a break and let life happen for a minute. I'll take a few deep breaths and usually, but not always, I'll accept the change, embrace it, and have fun with my dog for a little while, which will then trigger the happiness effect and, most likely, improve my writing. When life throws you a curveball, you might as well try to hit it out of the park. Change is inevitable and learning to use it to your advantage will bring you more happiness and abundance than you ever imagined.

Think about this: when your car gets in a rut, you push it out. Seems like common sense, right? However, when our lives get in a rut, we tend to say, "Life sucks" or "I'll just go with the flow and see what happens." But this will just make you stuck. Simply going with the flow down the river of life is not a good strategy; it will only lead to more of the same. You must steer your boat through the rapids, and you must figure out how to go around the large rocks that appear in front of you. You must embrace the newness of the change ahead and the challenges that change brings with it. You must also have a plan so that you can take positive action and take control of the changes. This will give you an abundance of confidence and will enable you to live your life fearlessly. I encourage you to look at any change in your life with passion and see how you can use the event to make your life better.

You cannot hide from changes in life. As a matter of fact, change is a law of the universe. It is the "law of rhythm," which says that all things rise and fall, everything is always in motion. Another universal law is the "law of polarity," or law of opposites, which states that everything is dual. For everything there is an opposite. To understand a tiny piece of the universal puzzle of life, I combine these two laws. You will soon begin to understand that you have some control over the experiences or perceived obstacles that are thrown your way. Let's see how this works for the benefit of our lives.

The law of polarity states that everything has an opposite: happy & sad, good & bad, hot & cold, etc. The law of rhythm states that everything has its tides: everything is constantly flowing in and out of change. What comes around, goes around in equal proportions. Visualize a pendulum swinging back and forth. Let's call one side of the pendulum the "good" side, and the other side will be the "bad" side. Now imagine that your life pendulum is swinging from good to bad and then back to good again. Your life is constantly in motion. Every good event will eventually be followed by a challenging event, which will then lead you back to a positive experience. This is how our life has been designed by the Creator, the Source, the Universe, God, or whatever you want to call it. Change is programmed into the universe, and you can activate the happiness effect by changing your perceptions.

Imagine that your life is the ball swinging on a pendulum. Label one side good and the other bad. On one end is what we perceive as a good experience, for instance walking on the beach. If we have a bad experience, for example we accidentally kick a rock, the pendulum will begin swinging to the opposite side. Suddenly, your current situation changes from good to bad.

Then the pendulum continues to swing to the bad side, because this is where you are focusing your attention. Next, you trip, fall, and get sand in your eyes. The pendulum has now swung to the far opposite side and is beginning its backswing. (It's a law, life must swing back!) The breeze blows the sand out of your eyes. Now, you are focused on the positive, happy feeling of being able to see again. The pendulum continues swinging forward to more goodness. And because you are focused on the good in your life once again, you just happen to find an old Spanish gold coin worth a thousand dollars. Your pendulum just swung from "good" to "great."

My theory is that had you been grateful for kicking the rock and seen that as a positive experience, you would have avoided getting sand in your eyes, and your pendulum would have skipped ahead to finding the gold coin. Your perception of events will override the pendulum, keeping it swinging from good to better. For many of you, your pendulum swings from bad to worse, because your perception of life blocks you from finding good in a given situation. By becoming aware of your negative perceptions of events, you can eliminate the negative experiences and focus your emotions only on the positive side of life.

One day a few years ago, I was driving my new truck home from work. Five minutes into my drive, I found myself stuck in a dead stop traffic jam on the interstate. I'd had a long day and just wanted to get home. I decided in a huff to take a side route; at least I would be moving. This is where my pendulum began moving to the negative side of life. I was so annoyed at having to take a detour that I was cursing to myself, focused on the negative.

As I came around a hairpin turn, the engine stopped, and the truck wouldn't move an inch. Luckily, I was able to get it to the shoulder, but it was now stuck on this dangerous curve. I was fuming at this point; there was no place in my mind for positive thoughts. I was letting my pendulum of life continue going negative. This is what many of us do throughout our lives. We allow outside negative influences to control every aspect of our life, never letting our life pendulum swing back to a positive experience.

Finally, I managed to contact a towing service, but I was still cursing and sending out negative thoughts. After about two hours of waiting for the tow truck, I finally settled down and began to see the humor in my situation. My wife arrived and we got to hang out and laugh about life for a while, something we were seldom able to do at the time. At this point I was feeling positive again. My pendulum was beginning to swing back.

After another hour went by, my truck was towed to the dealer. I had now accepted my defeat, and I started feeling good about my demise. The next morning my positivity remained high, and I was informed that my truck repairs were covered under the warranty, and I received three recall upgrades for free. I also had a tire that was going bad, and it was also covered under a warranty.

I'm not saying that all this good fortune happened because my attitude changed. However, it is another strange synchronicity that happened in my life. I also learned that getting upset was fruitless; life happens, and then it changes. Accept the change and see how you can embrace it in a positive way. The good will always return, and it will return sooner if you remain positive. Had I simply embraced and accepted my forced change, I may have avoided not only the breakdown but the three-hour wait as well. This is how you override the law of polarity – by turning the changes into a positive experience. You control your thoughts, so ultimately you control your satisfaction with life.

Here is a simple positivity exercise that you can use to overcome nearly all negative emotions. Today, find five minutes to be completely alone. Sit quietly and clear your mind. Now I want you to think back to your most perfect day. Do you remember how you felt, where you were, and who you were with? What smells and sounds did you experience? Now, let your body feel how good you felt that day. Let that happiness fill your mind and body. Sometimes I get the chills while doing this.

After a few minutes of focusing on this good feeling, go back to your life. The next time anything negative pulls you away from happiness, bring this feeling back to the front of your mind. Focus on that happy feeling until you can face your challenge with a positive mindset. When we break our connection to a thought pattern, we can instantly reverse direction. However, I will caution you that this works for both positivity and negativity. The key is to ensure you stay focused on the positive.

Have you ever had a day when things just kept going wrong? Imagine that you wake up and stub your toe. Then you slip in the shower. As you complain about how bad your morning is, you continue to experience unfortunate events. This is because our lives tend to go where our thoughts are focused. The opposite is also true. If you wake up and feel grateful (even if you stub your toe), you will continue to experience events to be grateful for. No matter how bad things get, there will always be a good event to focus on. You simply must look for it and be grateful.

A major factor in how satisfied we are with our lives is based on our perception of events. We control how we feel, react, and perceive everything that happens to us. We are in total control. Your pendulum of life never stops moving. The secret of maintaining happiness is to keep your pendulum swinging from good to better and from better to best!

Begin training your mind to see change as a good thing. No matter what happens in your life, find the good in it. When you can feel gratitude for both the good and the not so good events in your life, you will begin to see your life change for the better. As Tony Robbins put it, "You will notice that the changes, or challenges in life are happening *for* you, not *to* you." By controlling how you perceive life changes, you can rise above the pendulum swing. You can create a good experience in every situation. Your pendulum will always be swinging from good to better, and the bad will slowly disappear.

Today I can look back on my truck incident and realize that breaking down was happening *for* me, not *to* me. It allowed me to correct issues with the truck that I didn't even know about, and a dangerous tire was replaced, all for free. The universe was making sure I was safe. I was also provided with the perfect place to have uninterrupted time with my wife. Could the entire incident been designed by the universe to give my wife and I some quality time together? I will never know; however, I believe that the happiness effect is programmed into the universal laws of nature, and we simply must know how to use them.

Remember: you are what you think you are! When an unexpected expense pops up, you lose your job, or a family member or friend passes away, the experience can be an opportunity for you to learn how to find happiness. I'm not telling you to laugh at misfortune. However, you must take a moment – or sometimes a day or even a week – to accept the feeling and then move on because it is now behind you. You simply can't let adversity stop you from being happy. As you continue to practice the mindset tricks you've been taught, you will soon be able to actively wait for the pendulum to swing back to something better, knowing that prosperity and happiness always follow a downswing. The better you get at doing this, the happier and more abundant your life will be. Remember: you don't need a million dollars, you only need positive, grateful thoughts, and the rest will happen magically.

"Beliefs and thoughts alter cells in your body." - Bruce H. Lipton

24
YOU CONTROL YOUR CELLS

Your body is made up of billions of cells, and they are constantly changing. It is said that ninety percent of your cells are regenerated every seven to ten years. Only your cerebral cortex, your central nervous system, and heart muscle do not regenerate (https://askanaturalist.com/which-cells-are-never-replaced/). I think that may be because those systems keep our bodies doing what they do, directed by our subconscious mind. Without them, you might have to think about taking a breath or pumping blood. So, it is a good thing that they never change!

Ninety percent of you is new – or renewing – throughout your life. Think about that for a minute... That is amazing. You are not getting old! Your body is constantly renewing itself to keep you alive. Yes, as we age, some cells begin to renew less frequently, and eventually some cells stop being created. However, with the right diet, the right mindset, and some exercise, your body will stay in homeostasis for many, many years to come.

Your brain is so powerful that you don't have to think about basic life functions. Your mind does all the work behind the scenes. Your cells act based on your subconscious thoughts, which, to an extent, take orders from your conscious mind. For more details, check out Bruce Lipton's book *The Biology of Belief*, Gregg Braden's book *Spontaneous Healing*, or jump on the internet and do some research. If you tell yourself something long enough, with enough emotion, your subconscious will eventually believe it to be a fact. Your cells will then be directed by this new belief. That is how we are designed. In a way, it is like brainwashing.

This concept is similar to Pavlov's salivating dog experiment. Physiologist Ivan Pavlov studied the effects of stimulating dogs to elicit a learned response. In one experiment he would ring a bell and then feed the dogs. After some time of repeating this sequence, the dogs would begin salivating just from the sound of the bell. The dogs' bodies automatically reacted to the bell ringing, because their minds had been conditioned to respond to the sound. You can also condition your mind to always respond in a positive manner. With practice, your subconscious mind will take control and automatically assist you in turning negative experiences into positive journeys.

As you learn more things, your conscious mind pushes them to the subconscious, where they will always remain. This way you can focus on learning new things. You will always be able to call upon your subconscious mind for the information that you have given it. It's like riding a bike: once you can do it, you'll never forget how. You may need some time to re-acquire the forgotten behaviors, however, learned behaviors will likely appear when you need them. For example, when you see a red traffic light, you stop, as you have conditioned your mind to react in that specific way.

Just as you learn from your experiences, your cells do as well. When a virus gets into our bodies, our cells will attack it, because they have been programmed over millions of years to do just that. When we have an injury, our cells automatically begin the healing process without any conscious effort on our part, as they have been programmed to perform in this way. These cells are guided by our thoughts. Science is now studying how individual cells can make conscious decisions.

Now, this is where it gets cool. If you subconsciously control your cells, and your subconscious mind takes direction from your conscious thoughts, then you can heal your body through your thoughts. This is the placebo effect in action. There are numerous stories of miraculous healings that can only be attributed to the patient's state of mind. Professional athletes do this all the time. They focus their thoughts on their job and forget about the pain. If the pain returns after the game, many will visualize their bodies working at 100%, which can improve the healing process. Lance Armstrong, the famous cyclist, has stated many times that he used positive thoughts and visualization techniques to heal his cancer and to win races. He is one of many individuals who claim healing through their thoughts.

When I feel a cold coming on, I accept the feeling, I increase my consumption of anti-cold fruit, vegetables, and herbs, and then I mentally tell myself not to get sick. I have a saying that I will mentally repeat over and over until I believe it: "I am whole, I am perfect, I am strong, I am powerful, I am healthy, and I refuse to be sick. Cells, you need to return to balance and harmony; it's time to return to your normal cell line." I will focus on these thoughts until I'm feeling one hundred percent healthy. Using this technique, I have had only two days in the past six years when I felt somewhat sick for a whole day.

I know it's incredibly hard to focus on feeling good when your body is sick, however, if you want to speed up the healing process, thinking about feeling well and taking your mind away from the sickness or pain will drastically speed up the improvement of your condition. While I am repeating my mantra, I visualize my cells attacking and successfully eliminating the deformed cells. Whenever I feel like giving in to the "blah feeling" that colds produce, I mentally fight back reminding myself that I have the needed nutrients in my body, and I will not get sick. I haven't been knocked out sick in years.

If your conscious mind focuses on an area of your body, your cells will react. When you get sick or injured, and you want to feel better, your mind begins the healing process. However, you should be aware that the opposite is also true. If you focus on the pain, you will continue to feel pain. Whenever you think about buying some medicine or going to a doctor, these simple thoughts will get your cells' attention, and they will go into attack mode.

You must believe that you control your body. Belief is telling your cells that you're serious. If you have given your body the natural nutrients it needs, then your cells will heal you when you get sick, and you will heal faster if you believe that your cells can heal you. It is as simple as that.

Human beings have done extraordinary things when they have allowed their subconscious mind to take control. The mother who lifted a car to save her daughter, the man who healed his cancer and went on to win races, the blind who recovered their sight… All these people have proven that with positive thoughts and positive action, you can do anything. If you believe in an expected result and take intentional action to achieve those thoughts, you will receive the desired change. Change your thoughts, and you'll change your life.

Let's assume that you've had terrible back pain for years, and some days you can barely move. You have been to your doctor several times, and all they can do is perform surgery, which may cause you even worse damage. Of course, they can prescribe pain medications to ease your pain but fix nothing.

One day, you are slowly getting out of your chair. Your back is screaming in pain, and you can hardly stand up. Suddenly, your brand new thousand-dollar cell phone falls onto the concrete floor. You are filled with terror that you just destroyed your phone. You quickly stand up, bend completely over, and grab the phone off the ground. You see no cracks. *Ah*, a sigh of relief. You test all the buttons and fancy functions for ten minutes and everything is working great. *Ahhhhhhhhh*, super sigh of relief. Then you suddenly realize that you're standing straight, and you haven't thought about your back pain for the last twenty minutes. Then just as suddenly as you forgot about it, the pain returns, so you quickly sit back down and take some opium. (No judgement. As I revealed earlier, "been there, done that.")

How is it that for twenty minutes you had no pain? Not even a single thought of pain! But the minute you thought about your back, it was hurting again. BAM! the pain returned. Why?

If you can stop intense pain for a few seconds or minutes by being distracted, you can consciously feel less pain by focusing on something else! It may not always be easy, but if you can focus your attention anywhere but the pain, your pain will go away. I believe that to be a fact. Kids, hold your ears... When you're having sex, you feel zero pain, only pleasure. (If you're doing it right. Hehe.) Your headache goes away, your pain disappears, and you completely lose yourself in love, joy, and passion.

How does knowing that we control our cells help us find abundance? How can this knowledge help us activate the happiness effect? First and foremost, knowing that you are in total control of your body and mind should bring you an amazing amount of confidence. Believing in ourselves is a key component of creating a perfectly balanced and happy life. Use that confidence to build success in every area of your life.

When a challenge comes up, tell yourself that you will overcome it, and stay true to your desires. Find a way to see the positive lesson that the situation provides. If the challenge hurts or angers you, allow yourself to feel the pain. Working through your feelings may take some time, however, after acknowledging the pain as real, you need to go forward. Even in death we can find life lessons. While reflecting on how someone lived their life and what we can learn from them, death becomes a growing experience, and we, like nature, are here to grow. Can you take something from the deceased's life experiences and make your life better? If you open your mind and allow the answers to come, they will. You will be amazed at how fast and easily you can overcome adversity and begin moving forward again.

Our brains are incredibly powerful; we simply must guide them and then step aside, letting them do their magic. When you are maintaining positive thoughts, and you have trained your mind to be grateful while seeing the good in all events in your life, you will reach your goals and live a life of abundance. Your happiness will be contagious. You will start to notice that other people will want to be around you. You will attract happiness to you as well as spread it to others. You will be able to create your perfect life because you control your level of happiness with your thoughts.

"Acknowledging the good that you already have in your life is the foundation for all abundance." - Eckhart Tolle

25
GRATITUDE FEELS GOOD

We have learned about change and how you cannot hide from it. You must embrace change, as only you control how it will affect you. Everything always works out in the end, so be patient and plan for the next good beginning. You can even speed up the downswing so that the good begins happening faster. How, you ask? By feeling and showing gratitude.

Part of being successful in this life is being grateful for everything you have and everything you want to have, with no strings attached. When you wake up, say thank you to your body and mind. While you slept last night, your mind kept you breathing. It kept your heart beating and your blood flowing. Your liver took up and converted toxins that you picked up during the day. Your kidneys processed waste. Your stomach turned food into energy. Your body made sure you would wake up healthier than you were when you went to sleep. You are a new you every single day. That is something to be grateful for!

I am not a doctor, so I don't know everything the body does in a scientific way. I just know some basic common-sense stuff. Your body and mind have your back – they make you a better person overnight. You don't have to do anything other than fall asleep. You must be thankful for that amazing blessing from the universe. You get a better life and a better body, and all that is asked in return from you is to be grateful, and of course, sleep once a day.

During my transformation I learned about the importance of gratitude. I began a gratitude journal – every night before going to sleep and then immediately after waking up, I would list three to five reasons to be grateful. My list got to be over 300 entries by the time I stopped listing them. Today I will only list something new that really stands out, as I am frequently thankful for the same blessings in my life.

When you are grateful for what you have, the universe responds with more of what you're thankful for. It's that simple. For instance, if you are grateful for being able to pay your bills, you will not only be able to pay your bills, but you will usually have money left over. When you begin to be thankful for this leftover money, even if it is only fifty cents, your prosperity will increase. The way I see it, if your needs are met, you are living in abundance.

You can either become a "glass half full" (positive) person or a "glass half empty" (negative) person. The choice is yours. You can choose to see the leftover fifty cents after paying bills as an abundant windfall and gratefully celebrate your good fortune, or you can be ungrateful and disappointed that you only have fifty cents. I can confirm that when your attitude is full of gratitude, your finances will improve. If you are complaining about your small paycheck or lack of money, you will soon have more things to complain about. If you want to get rich, start being grateful for what you already have today!

I began being thankful that I had enough money to pay my bills, even if there was no money left for fun things. After a couple of months of practicing this, I began noticing minor shifts in my life. My bank account seemed to always have money in it when I needed it. My 401(K) started to really do well, and sometimes money would just show up. Financial writer Ken Honda states that you must show "arigato," or gratitude, for your money, both as it comes in and as it goes out. This has worked in my life, and I believe it will work for you too.

One year my family really needed a fun break, but we didn't have the money for a vacation. However, I began visualizing how nice a family vacation would be. I was thankful that we could start planning it even without the funds. After about two months of intentionally thinking about taking a family trip, out of the blue my dad asked if we could use some money to take a trip to St. Louis to see the family. The money he offered us, along with what we had saved, was just enough to cover a week's stay at a nice hotel. It was perfect, unexpected, and showed me how the universe repays your gratitude.

If you are hoping for more abundance, show more gratitude. Become grateful for what you already have. You will begin to see the abundance of food in your refrigerator you didn't see before. You will see the abundance of clothing you already have, and you will see that you always have money left over. You must be truly, emotionally grateful, then watch what happens. That simple shift from being grateful for having enough, to being grateful for having more than enough, will begin to change your life. It will ensure that your dreams become your reality.

"If humans were to model the lifestyle displayed by a healthy community of cells, our societies and our planet would be more peaceful and vital." - Bruce H. Lipton

26
COMMUNITIES AND SOCIAL LIFE

Another great secret to a happy and healthy life is that you need to have a social life. I am not talking about partying all night at the clubs. I am referring to having friends, family or just a neighbor to talk to occasionally. We need to have social interaction with other people in a positive way. Even being social with coworkers or the cashier at the grocery store will help you if that's your only connection to people.

Whether you are religious or not, it seems that our need for companionship all started with Adam and Eve. As God said, "It is not good for the man to be alone." (Genesis 2:18) And we are not alone with our need for social interaction; atoms, molecules, even our cells all needed to form communities to form bigger and more complex structures.

It seems that most things in nature, including you, cannot successfully live without interacting with others. Like us, many plants also need to belong to a community. Some plants need the bees and butterflies to pollinate their flowers, or fruit won't form, and they can't reproduce. Trees and other plants depend on birds, animals and even humans to spread their seeds far and wide, ensuring that the genus survives.

What is more, science is currently proving that plants can communicate with each other. Some plants speak through their roots, while other plants release chemicals to draw attention to danger. Everything in nature needs a community to support it. Can it even be an undiscovered law of the universe? We could call it Steve's Law of Community.

When you are part of a community, you fill the gaps in your life through interacting with other people. Your experiences help you grow, and experiences that you have with others can help them grow as well. We need each other to become more balanced people.

Some of you may consider yourselves introverts, possibly even having anxiety attacks simply thinking about interacting with others. That's okay, this is a quite common fear. I have never been incredibly open with people that I'm unfamiliar with. This is an area of my life that I must work on every day. Today, when I am out in public, I remind myself that (1) the world is happening *for* me, and I am looking forward to the journey; (2) I need to set an intention to be positive with the people I meet; and (3) that when I do have to interact with someone I don't know, I need to try to intently listen to them and enjoy their story. This usually helps me relax. Focusing on and intently listening to others will make the conversation more personal, as you are now taking an active interest in another person. This simple exchange will create the happiness effect in both of you.

Think about the cells in your body: they are individuals, but they need other cells to make you whole; they must cooperate to make your body work. It's the same with people: a community helps one another, which benefits everyone as well as the community as a whole.

I have lived in South Florida for over 25 years. I have been through about ten hurricanes, and twice the eye of the storm passed directly overhead. Prior to the storm's arrival many people are in panic mode. They become focused solely on their needs, blocking out everything else. Tempers can flare as anxiety and the fear of possible harm take control of their thoughts. You can feel the panic in the air, and when you walk into a store full of scared people, it can be a little unnerving.

However, once the storm has passed, and the fear begins to subside, we all creep out of our houses to survey the damage. Everyone seems concerned about their neighbors. People I had never met before will ask, "Are you okay? Do you need any help?" Those with chainsaws will begin cutting tree limbs to clear a path until government crews can get to the neighborhood. Others will help move debris to central piles. Still others will check on the elderly.

Every storm I have experienced has ended the same way. The community comes together and ensures everyone is okay. I have made some good friends because of the bonding and camaraderie that take place while helping each other during a time of need. I must also say that I seldom see news stories regarding our communities coming together. I feel the media is misleading the public into believing life is full of bad luck. If they ran more positive stories, maybe the world would become a more positive place for everyone. (More on this later.)

A community could be you, your mom, and dad; it could also be you, the checkout person at the store, and the postman. (I really like my postman; he is a cool guy. When I have time, we'll talk for several minutes about life. When we're done, I feel uplifted. He is part of my community.) Your community may be your neighborhood, your city, or your state. Large or small doesn't seem to matter, but we all need social interaction.

I'm not completely convinced, though, that your million friends on Facebook qualify as a community in this sense. You can create an amazing support group or a thriving virtual community on social media, however, we also need face-to-face interaction with other people to achieve a completely balanced life. As Bette Midler sang, "Ya gotta have friends." She was more right than she knew!

Understanding how a community works together for the betterment of all members helps us visualize how our cells form a well-functioning community as well. A community will come together in time of need to help one of its own, just like nature and your cells do. A community will come together to fight off dangers. A community will come together in celebration. (I don't know if our cells celebrate, but I believe they do.) For a community to thrive, it needs positive reinforcement from the members, just like nature and your cells do.

Your cells work together to make you a perfect you. If they get the nutrients and positive reinforcement they need, your cells will constantly interact with each other to ensure a healthy body. They band together to help and support each other throughout their lives. They join forces to provide nutrients to your body to fight off germs. If cancer or toxins enter your body, and you have created a positive, nutrient-rich environment by eating and medicating naturally, your cells will attack the cancer and cut off its supply of food. When your cells are working together in homeostasis, your body and mind will also thrive.

I think this is a good time to tell you one of the biggest secrets for igniting the happiness effect in your life. If you think you can handle it now. Turn the page to find out.

"Journalism largely consists of saying, 'Lord Jones is dead' to people who never knew Lord Jones was alive." - G. K. Chesterton

27
STOP WATCHING THE NEWS!

Why do you watch the news? I think I know what you are going to say: because you need to know what's happening in the world. But why do you need to know what is going on in China or Africa or Egypt every day? Are you going to do anything about it? Nope! Why do you care what the name of a kid who was shot in Chicago is if you live in Miami or anywhere else for that matter? Why do you get upset about any political issue that the news anchor talks about? Will you do anything with that frustration? Will you call your congressperson? Will you volunteer to improve or change the situation? Will you do anything other than make yourself unhappy?

Most likely, you will complain to your coworkers and friends. You will not be discussing solutions or positive actions that you will take. You will be solely focused on feeding your negative emotions the entire day. Then, after a long day of negativity, you go home and complain to your family while watching more news, making your home life unbearable as well. You are unknowingly killing yourself and those around you!

I know this is true for many of you because that used to be me. The television was on 24/7, because I thought I needed to know what was going on. For most of my life I would wake up and turn on a news program while getting ready for my day. I would be listening to all the misery in the world, priming myself for a day of negativity. The traffic announcer would instruct me that the drive would be hectic and filled with delays. The meteorologist threatened me with weather that was too hot, too cold, too wet, and the anchors filled my head with impending doom. Even on a payday, a day to celebrate, I would complain to my coworkers about how little my check was, how the economy was getting worse, the president didn't do his job, and China or Russia hated me. This is what the news was teaching.

In the meantime, my life was totally fine. I had enough money to pay the bills, I had a home, a car, a great family. Abundance was all around me, but I couldn't see it. I was allowing a news program to convince me that my world was falling apart, and I should be fearful of my future. I would then believe the news and spend my days complaining, drinking alcohol, popping pills and never truly being happy. This not only affected me, but it would also bring others down to my level of misery. Remember: A community needs positive reinforcement, but the news reinforces negative attitudes, which will eventually destroy your community, so please turn off the news.

A study by researchers Shawn Achor and Michelle Gielan, along with Thrive-founder Arianna Huffington found that just three minutes of negative news in the morning (versus more uplifting content) can ruin your mood for the rest of the day. Now think about this: what if you're watching four, eight, or twelve hours of news every day? You will never be happy!

This seems like a good time to point out that negativity hurts your three Life Centers. The news breeds anger, stress, fear, anxiety, worry, and depression, which all create problems for your body. Stress affects your cardiovascular and digestive systems, which will eventually reduce your ability to think rationally. Depression is rampant in America and is in the annual top ten causes of death every year. Maybe, we should hold the news accountable.

I used to believe that news anchors were always telling the truth because they cared. Well, they mostly don't. Most news anchors are communications majors or drama students who are paid to entertain you, not give you facts. They are paid to convincingly read a script that was designed to elicit negative emotions from the viewers. Have you ever heard the phrase "If it bleeds, it leads"? This is the motto of news organizations around the world. It doesn't matter if the stories are relevant to our lives, it is only about keeping you glued to the screen, because that's how they make money.

Many news anchors have little experience with world events or the global economy; they had no idea where Bangladesh or Pyongyang was until their producer brought them their script. I don't mean to sound harsh, but the people who know about world affairs are the people making the news, not reporting on it. You should also be aware that many news anchors simply want to be a celebrity on TV, and you don't get to be a celebrity if you only talk about boring facts. They must trigger your emotions, and negative emotions will keep you watching.

Your favorite news station, whether it be liberal, conservative, or independent (although I personally don't know of a mainstream truly independent news station) is not telling you all the facts, because that would be boring, and there is no money in boring TV. Real news should be fact-based, not opinion based. However, news anchors are paid to give you opinions and many times forget to tell you the facts. Politicians are also great at this.

Your emotions help to keep you glued to the TV. The names of the victims and the perpetrators are given so that you feel like you knew them. This way, TV stations make the news personal even when it's not. This tactic keeps you glued to the story, even though the story has no direct impact on your life. Thus, you will keep watching, even staying tuned during the commercials. Advertising is the driving force behind the news, as this is how the stations make money and pay salaries.

But I have news (ha-ha) for you: knowing the names of the victims helps no one, and it's none of your business anyway. It only brings more sorrow, negativity, and fear into your life. Why do you care if the victim's name is Timmy? He will still be a stranger to you! Yes, it is heart-wrenching to hear of a child's death. However, what gets accomplished by you knowing their name? If you are not one of the victim's acquaintances, you will not be affected by the story unless you allow the media to drive your emotions. This mass personalization of negativity is simply one of many unhealthy aspects of watching the news or television in general.

The news also does its best to sway public opinion, just like in the 1930s, when Randolph Hearst had his newspapers run false anti-cannabis stories. Today's news outlets are trying to make you believe whatever the station owners want you to believe. The producers are directed to only talk positively about one side of the issue. I have never seen a non-biased news report in my life. Have you?

The station owners decide what the facts are, based on their political and business objectives and beliefs. The news stations then spice it up with cool graphics of death and destruction to keep you entertained. The news is designed to instill fear and worry into your lives, because when you're scared, you can be controlled.

Here's another example: As hurricanes barrel towards land, the media begins warning viewers of the impending doom weeks in advance. They will provide graphics of past destruction and charts with possible landfalls, knowing that a storms trajectory can drastically change from day to day. This early over-reporting ensures the broadest audience possible. Once a headline declares a possible landfall, millions will be glued to the television for weeks absorbing nothing but fear and negativity. Yes, those of us living in storm zones need to be aware of potential storms, but a quick check with NOAA.org will show you all the information you need without the fear and worry. If you live in a hurricane zone, there is absolutely no excuse for not having enough basic supplies on hand to survive for three days. This is something all of us should do. When you know that you have a plan, and you are prepared to execute that plan, you are free to focus on what truly matters: positivity. We certainly don't need the extra negative emotions that the media provides in these instances. Be prepared, have a plan, and do not worry!

To be fair to the news anchors and media giants around the world, I must let you in on another secret. Your brain is hardwired to be addicted to negative news. It is called the "negativity bias." This condition was part of what created the fight or flight response in prehistoric humans, who needed to be super aware of negative influences in their environment or they would not survive. Although today we have fewer reasons to use our fight or flight senses, negative news does trigger the reaction.

Negative news is just as addictive as opioid drugs and probably kills just as many people (my opinion, never proven). When hearing negative news, your brain releases dopamine – the same chemical that makes you feel good when taking opioids, alcohol, and nicotine. Dopamine contributes to your addiction because your body is conditioned to want more. You are physically addicted to the news, and not just any news, nope, only negative news. I will give news anchors a break; they are only doing what they are paid to do. *You* are the one to blame. *You* are the one addicted.

Have you ever noticed that during a half hour news program, there is usually a three-minute feel-good segment? That is because it gives you hope and lets your mind relax. The feel-good moment stops the flow of dopamine in your brain, which helps calm you down. Too much negativity could overload your brain, similarly to a drug overdose. However, they won't show too many happy stories because there is no money in it. The news station goes back to negativity because it pays their salaries.

If you need to stay up to date on the hot issues of the day, sign up for an internet news service or use Google News and read the headlines. If something catches your attention, read the whole article. Then search for four more articles on the same story from opposing viewpoints, and only then make your judgment. Don't rely on your buddy at work who claims to know everything about politics or the economy. Don't rely on a political party that will only share their side of the story with you. Don't rely on your favorite news entertainer who is just as clueless as you are.

If you really need that negative news fix, focus on community issues which you can get involved in. Learn what's going on around you. By working on improving your community, you will turn your need for negativity into a positive experience.

Also, stop listening to celebrities' and athletes' opinions. Game playing and acting does not make anyone an expert on world affairs! Money and fame are not requirements for intelligence. I know that some famous people are extremely smart. However, most are not world affair experts. They certainly have no understanding of your immediate circumstances, which are most likely not the same as theirs. They may be great actors, athletes, or musicians, but they should not be the voice you listen to for news that affects you.

When you stop following the herd and turn off the news, you will become the leader. You will build confidence by following your own path, and you will become the expert on the facts. However, you must do your own research and begin to form your own opinions. As you work through finding the facts yourself, not relying on the news for your information, you will soon realize that life is actually incredibly positive. Soon you will become the happiest, healthiest, and smartest person in the room.

"We only have one life, but we can choose what kind of story it's going to be." - Rick Riordan

28
REWRITING YOUR STORY

Another great secret to a positive, happy life is to clear out negative feelings from your past. Your brain has stored every emotion you have ever had. All the stories from your past, both the good and the not so good, have been recorded in your subconscious mind, and all those emotions are still directing your life today. Are you being guided by past negativity that continues to play out in the present and will steer your future as well? Or is your emotional library filled with happiness, gratitude, learning, growing, and abundance?

Your past emotions are sometimes buried beneath a lot of garbage and false beliefs. You will have to throw away some of the fake stories you've been telling yourself if you want to rewrite your history. For you to be filled with consistent happiness, you must find the good in all past experiences even if you don't view your life story as all roses and unicorns. I have shared with you my $8000 loss and how I finally overcame that experience, but I have had many other situations in my life that would haunt me until I reversed the perception that I had.

In my freshman year of high school, I tried out for the basketball team. I had played and started on elite travel teams prior to this and felt that making the team would be easy. I practiced and worked hard, making it to the final cut day. But on the night before the final practice, I chose to go out with some older friends and party, knowing that it was not a good idea. On the final day of tryouts, I missed several easy shots, and I was not playing full out. I was beaten by slower players at almost every drill. I was justly cut from the team; however, I blamed the coach and school politics for cutting me. I held this belief well into adulthood.

The false story I told myself was directing my life in a negative way. I learned that I could always blame someone or something for all the problems in my life. I seldom accepted responsibility for my actions and blamed most failures on outside influences. To live a more positive lifestyle, I had to revisit many stories like this that I had been telling myself for years. I can now admit that I was the culprit in not being selected. I chose to drink and stay out late instead of focusing on the task at hand.

Since then, my perception has changed, and I have rewritten my story. I know that I made a poor choice, and that choice was 100% mine. From this one incident, I learned that whatever we want in life can be ours, we simply must make wise choices. If we choose the un-wise path, we must accept our choices, find a positive solution, and then move forward. Today I try to see the ramifications of my decisions before I make them.

We've all had days, or even years, when things were tough. Maybe you lost your job or your house. Maybe you feel a family member did you wrong, and you can't forgive them. Maybe you had a loved one pass away. These can all be devastating to our present lives. But remember you are not alone. Every human being has been hit by tough times, and most of us get through them fine. The people who understand that life must change for the better and plan their recovery will get through the challenges with ease. As you learn to accept your decisions and begin turning old events into positive experiences, you will be able to overcome any negative feelings that you have ever had.

Only you have the power to rewrite your story the way you want it to be told. That's extremely exciting and should have you jumping for joy. You are in total control of your life, past, present, and future, and you control how you want to perceive it all. I know you can do this because you are here, reading this book, and things are about to get a lot better for your life!

You need to look back on your life and replay every single memory with a happy ending. Let's say your parents left you when you were eight years old, sending you to foster care. This made you feel unloved your whole life, and you are still blaming every challenge you face on that experience. Now, when you replay your life, you realize that you met your best friend in foster care, and you are still as close as ever. Certainly, losing our parents at a young age is devastating, and many people would see that as an excuse for giving up or accepting mediocrity. However, when you realize that the adversity made you stronger, the whole experience changes into a positive adventure. If you shift your perception of events, they become lucky occasions that have changed your life for the best.

For you to be successful, look back over your life and begin seeing every moment as having a positive outcome. Sometimes these memories have been buried for years, and we don't want to bring them to the surface again. They may make you face fears you don't even know you have. But to re-imagine your life and create the happiness effect that will last, you will need to be fearless. You must face your perceived negative experiences and replay them in a positive way until you can *feel joy* when you think about them. The only way to reach a completely happy and balanced life is to view your life as lucky, positive, and abundant.

After you spend some time rewriting your life history with only positive twists, you will begin to wonder why you saw some events as horribly negative at the time. Yes, they were challenging, but you have overcome them with determined positivity, even if you didn't know it at the time.

As you rewrite more and more of your life stories, you will begin to connect the dots that make up your life picture. You will notice that the perceived negative experiences created a learning environment, allowing you to grow and be a more confident person. Remember: What doesn't kill you makes you stronger. Every single experience, no matter how bad you feel it was, made you a better person. I didn't make the basketball team, which then allowed me to try out for soccer. I made that team and made a lot of new friends in the process. Looking back on it, everything worked out simply fine, like it always does.

As you practice more and try to experience your past life as a happy, good, growing experience, you will begin feeling a sense of joy, optimism, and happiness. When you look back on your past and see how it really was all good, you will be confident that your life will always be all good. As the happiness effect takes hold, your new, positive mindset will bring you abundance with little effort on your part! It is like magic.

Many of you may feel overwhelmed at the thought of changing a family member's death into a positive experience. I agree that it sounds daunting. However, as you begin shifting to a happiness mindset, you will become more experienced and comfortable replaying past events in a positive way. Like everything in life and in nature, it takes a little patience and intentional daily practice.

One effective way to begin seeing the positive side of things while increasing your gratitude towards life is to use a "gratitude charm." You simply need an object such as a rock, a pin, or some talisman to hold at night before going to bed. I use a polished rock that was in the bucket I grew my first turmeric in, because I am grateful for that experience. While holding your gratitude charm, replay the events of the day and say thank you for all the good that happened that day. You can say it out loud or silently in your mind, whatever makes you feel the gratitude more fully. Go through your entire day and replay all the events so that each one ends positively. You must even re-live your negative experiences, then look for the good that came from them. There is always a positive attached to the negative, you simply must find it, and with practice, you will.

At first you may need to carry your gratitude charm with you throughout the day. When negativity rears its ugly head, simply touching or holding your charm will force you to begin thinking grateful thoughts. It will assist you in overcoming negativity. If you have difficulty feeling grateful for your day due to only seeing it as negative, remember that if you learned something new, even if it was painful, it will have a positive effect on your life, as it forces you to grow. And just like nature, we need to be always growing.

I should also let you know that how you start your day will dictate how your day will go. Instead of waking up with negative news, emails, or doubts and worries, wake up with gratitude. If three minutes of negative news can ruin your whole day, just imagine what five minutes of being thankful can do! When you wake up, take a few minutes, and just say thank you for whatever comes to mind. Setting your day up with gratitude will drastically improve how your day is experienced.

If seeing reasons to be grateful is a challenge for you, then I suggest a gratitude journal. I have created *The 30-Day Gratitude Challenge* journal for this purpose. You can find it on my website (Stephentradentz.com). However, you could simply use a notepad or a diary app on your phone. Every day for the next thirty days think of three or more reasons to be grateful. You can do this anytime during the day; whenever something comes to mind, take a minute to appreciate the feeling and then write it down in your journal. The act of writing your gratitude thoughts down cements that feeling in your mind. Soon, you will be blown away by how much abundance there already is all around you. Start and end your days with gratitude. The more you do this, the faster your life will become consistently happy.

As you begin to see the abundance that is already provided for you, and you learn to be grateful for every experience, rewriting your life's history will become stress free. When a challenge hits you in the present and you replay it in a positive way that evening, you will begin to see new ways of reviewing your past as well. Practice makes perfect, but you should not force it. Try to make it a fun activity. Learn to laugh at yourself, your life, and the driver who just cut you off.

SECTION 8

FINAL THOUGHTS

"Live the life of your dreams. When you start living your dream life there will always be obstacles, doubters, mistakes, and setbacks. But with hard work, perseverance, and belief there is no limit to what you can achieve." - Roy T. Bennett

29
FINAL REVIEW

A very important part of creating the happiness effect is belief. If you don't believe you can be happy, you won't be. It's that simple. It doesn't matter what religion or spiritual views you follow; they all tell you that you need to believe. Belief is at the center of our lives.

Every time you take a step, you subconsciously believe your next foot is coming right along. You believe that when you step outside, there will be oxygen to breathe. You unquestionably believe that when you go to sleep, you will wake up. That is the kind of belief that you need to have. If you are the one who can control your feelings, and you know that you are in control of your thoughts, then you can believe in a happy, carefree life filled with prosperity. If you unquestionably believe that your life is happy, balanced, and positive, abundance will follow. This is how the universe is designed.

When I began feeling abundance for the little money left over from paying bills, I believed that more abundance would follow, and it has. I didn't just start being grateful because I thought it would make me feel good; the main reason for believing was to increase my financial abundance. I believed that I could create an abundant life, and it is happening every day.

When we started our journey together, you learned that you have been "played" by the American healthcare system. You now know that the largest agriculture, pharmaceutical, and chemical companies work together to keep you using their synthetic products that may be killing you. You know that insurance can also be a scam that keeps you losing money and harming your health. If your insurance company were really concerned for your health, they would provide insurance benefits that included inexpensive organic foods as well.

Refined sugar, high amounts of sodium, as well as the synthetic chemicals from fertilizers, herbicides, and pesticides that are used when growing GMO crops are found in many commercially processed and packaged foods. These have been connected to an increased risk of cancer. You have learned that fruit, vegetables, and herbs all affect the three Life Centers of your body, and that eating a variety of colors of each every day will allow your body to become balanced. Your diet determines your mind, which sets up your life. You must:

Get your body right
To get your mind right
To get your life right.

If your body doesn't have a variety of natural nutrients, your mind will never be one hundred percent balanced. If you are eating commercially packaged and processed foods and taking prescription drugs, your body's puzzle will never fit together perfectly. Synthetic food and drugs will always create unnatural and unexpected results in our bodies. You will then have to take more synthetic products to try and fix what you've changed.

Now you know how cannabis and hemp are found in nature and how they specifically target our body's endocannabinoid system. These amazing plants have over one hundred beneficial nutrients including cannabinoids that can heal as well as maintain your body. The nutrients in the cannabis plant will contribute to your body's homeostasis.

There has never been a documented death caused by cannabis,

yet it is still mostly illegal. Opioids kill over 40,000 people every year, and our American healthcare system kills over 400,000 people every year as well. Maybe cannabis and hemp could reduce those numbers, only time will tell.

I have said it many times since we started our journey together that life is about becoming balanced, not perfect. That is a cool part of what I'm teaching. You get to be you. Imperfections are natural and should be expected. If you were perfect, you would be abnormal! We all make mistakes, and now that you have read this book, you know that mistakes are simply accomplishments waiting to happen. You know that finding the good in every situation will make you a winner.

You know that happiness is within your grasp because you control your emotions. You know that challenges will pop up, but you also know that after a challenge, life must get better. The law of rhythm and the law of duality dictate that change must be a part of your life. If you are looking for the good during challenging times, better days will soon return, and then you can take additional action to maintain your positive momentum.

With your positive mindset, you can control your pendulum so that it swings from good to better, and then from better to best. Your positive perception of life will assist you in avoiding the negative experiences that life brings your way. You will always create a good outcome because you know that everything always works out.

You simply must try to have a positive attitude. Every time you react negatively to events in your life, you are contributing to your cells' death, and you are attracting more negativity into your life. You must work on turning negativity into positivity. Turn that frown upside down – this is a cornerstone for your consistent happiness. Another cornerstone is gratitude. You must be grateful for everything that is in your world. It is impossible to be sad or mad when you are feeling grateful. This is a scientific fact: gratitude replaces negativity every time.

You are a new you every day! That's something to be grateful for! Your cells will follow your lead. If you have given them a nutrient-rich environment and they are filled with positivity, they will provide you with perfect health for many years. If you believe that you can succeed, you will. You can have a perfect, abundant, healthy, and happy life. It is all up to you!

"Happiness is the highest form of health." - Dalai Lama

30
PUTTING IT ALL TOGETHER

Congratulations! You have made it to the end of our journey together. The secrets to good health and happiness are within your grasp. You can release any fear or worries that you had about life. When you feel that sudden, sickening gush of nausea in your stomach because you don't know how you will pay the next bill, stop and relax. Take thirty seconds and breathe deeply. Sometimes you may need more than thirty seconds, but that's okay. Close your eyes and remind yourself that *everything always works out*. Walk away from any negative issues in your life, then ask the universe for a solution. If you have followed and put into practice all that we've discussed, you will find the answer.

It took me over two years to write this book. Several times I was ready to throw in the towel and give up. When I would get in a funk, I would step away from writing, close my eyes and try to clear my mind. I would say to the universe, "I want to inspire people to feel more happiness, and I know you will help guide my words so that others will understand." Sometimes I could start writing right away, other times it would take a day or two. But as soon as I let my mind clear, writing could begin again. The universe wants us to succeed, we simply must ask, believe, act, then get out of the way and allow it to happen for us.

When you release all your fears and worries and believe that your life is good, a solution will be provided to you by the universe. It will simply pop into your mind. Once you receive a feeling to move in a certain direction, you must act. By taking action you are affirming the universe, or God, that this is the direction you desire to go. Your action completes the cycle, and now the universe will begin providing more experiences that will guide you toward your dreams. This works every time! As it is stated in the Bible, "Ask, believe, receive."

Your body knows what it needs, so listen to the signals it gives you. Remember, the gut feeling you have is a message coming from your three Life Centers through your connection to the universe. I'm not saying that our gut feelings are always right, however, in my experience, not listening to your gut might lead you down some dark paths. Prior to ending up in the hospital with a bleeding ulcer, I was given many little clues from the universe to stop abusing pharmaceutical drugs. My head, chest, and gut all tightened up several times as I went to refill my prescription, and a tiny voice in my head reminded me that it was bad for my body. I consistently ignored these feelings until I had to face the fact that if I wanted to live, I would have to change.

The minute I committed to changing, the universe began providing me with opportunities for improvement. I met a holistic doctor who began my quest for a better life. I learned about natural food and medicine, while positive thought mentors began showing up in my day-to-day activities. Eventually, I was led to writing this book and helping you.

It can be hard to listen to your inner voice, but if you choose to ignore your gut, I can guarantee you that the universe will eventually punch you in the face to make you listen. It's much easier to listen to our feelings and act before we are forced to do it.

You are part of nature, and nature knows how to succeed. You simply must believe in yourself. The solutions for success are designed right into you. Nature provides for your needs in abundance. The tools that you need to experience a healthy and happy life are already right in front of you. You must open your eyes and mind to see the abundance around you. It really is everywhere.

I believe that everything in this world has a purpose. Everything and everyone must work together, just like your three Life Centers work together to make you whole. If one center is not being taken care of, it will lead to the destruction of your other two, eventually leading to a slow, painful death. The same is true of nature. If we wipe out a species, it will negatively affect all other parts of the planet. The universe has been put together in an amazingly balanced way, like our body. Everything relies on everything else. Just like our bodies, the universe can handle a lot of abuse and still recover, however, if we keep creating negative impacts, our bodies, the planet, and the universe will eventually give up and die.

Remember that you control how you feel. Keep the positive thoughts flowing to find the happiness and abundance that you desire. Continue learning and keep researching everything. Before you know it, you will become an expert in natural health and positive momentum. People will want to hear your story, and you will help others activate their own happiness effect.

You must believe that you are the best you that you can be. See it clearly in your mind and never stop dreaming. Belief in your dreams holds the key to your future.

Hakuna Matata.

OTHER BOOKS BY STEPHEN T RADENTZ:

Balanced Life Daily Planning Journal
https://stephentradentz.com/products/a-balanced-life-daily-planning-journal

30-DAY Gratitude Challenge Journal
https://stephentradentz.com/products/30-day-gratitude-challenge-journal

All books can be found on my website
https://Stephentradentz.com

Or my blog:
https://Balancedbynature.net

Below are the kindle links for my plant health benefit booklets.

5 Herbal Tea Blends to Balance Your Life

Stephen T's Ultimate Smoothie

Medical Marijuana The Simple Truth

THANK YOU!

Thank you so much for reading! I truly hope you enjoyed it, and found your path to a better life. As a small token of gratitude, I'd like to send you a free bonus: *The First Steps System to Happiness and Health*. This free bonus includes:

1. 5 herbal teas recipe booklet (with pictures of herbs, NOT in the printed version).
2. Ultimate smoothie recipe booklet (with pictures of herbs, NOT in the printed version).
3. A quick reference chart of 50 herbs and their health benefits.
4. Daily, weekly, and monthly pages and initial health assessment pages from the Balanced Life Daily Planning Journal which can be printed out and used to create your own journal.
5. A 10% off coupon code for any purchase on my website.

I'm excited to give you this $50 value for FREE as a THANK YOU for reading my book and supporting my work. You'll also be notified of any pending book releases, events, or updated content.

What are you waiting for?

Sign up now: StephenTRadentz.com/products/bonus-offer

Thanks so much for choosing to go on this journey with me. Authors need and appreciate support from folks like you, and I hope you continue in your journey to natural health and happiness. Please don't hesitate to connect with me if you have any questions about the book.

Steve@stephentradentz.com

I enjoy connecting with readers and would love to hear from you!

Thanks again,

—Stephen T Radentz

www.ingramcontent.com/pod-product-compliance
Lightning Source LLC
Chambersburg PA
CBHW072157100526
44589CB00015B/2260